THE
MEDIUMS
HANDBOOK

THE MEDIUMS HANDBOOK

REV. GORDON M BROMLEY

authorHOUSE®

AuthorHouse™
1663 Liberty Drive
Bloomington, IN 47403
www.authorhouse.com
Phone: 1-800-839-8640

Published by AuthorHouse   08/25/2012

ISBN: 978-1-4772-2655-1 (sc)
ISBN: 978-1-4772-2656-8 (e)

TABLE OF CONTENTS

FOREWORD

I have known Gordon for many years now; we first met when Gordon and his wife Eve became founding members of The Haymist physical circle of which I was the medium. As time progressed in the development of the Haymist circle, Gordon assumed the role of circle leader, a role that he excelled at.

Gordon has many years experience in the field of mediumistic and spiritual understanding and is best suited to pen a book upon this varied and diverse subject. Being a certificated medium and healer and ordained Minister he has first hand experience of most if not all of the subjects covered in this book.

The Mediums Handbook is an easy to read book, for it contains a wealth of knowledge, which is close to hand. Any person reading this book will not fail to notice the quality of information and the painstaking research that was undertaken to make this book interesting for people looking to understand a little more about the subject matter or to further their own knowledge.

Note: The references in this book are from the authors own personal experience and understanding, not myself.

David Thompson (May 2012) Physical Medium

INTRODUCTION

The aim of this book is to clearly and simply explain aspects of Spiritualism to the novice, and also to be a reference book for mediums that have a degree of understanding and just require specific information. Many people, with differing intellects and cultures, from various and different psychic and spiritual development levels and walks of life, over the years, have asked questions relating to spiritualism. Hopefully the answers will be contained in this book. It needs to be stressed that I am an imperfect soul, and that I do not know everything. I am still learning, and will continue to do so even when I pass to the spirit world.

If one considers the complete spectrum of mediumship, and then try and write it in a book, volumes could be written. This book is not only intended as a basic tutorial but also as a reference book. It also gives personal views of the author. No responsibility is taken for using the information contained herein, if problems arise. Each person should combine common sense with any given instructions.

Much has been said and written about the development of mediums, some of it good, some mediocre and some useless. Many people set themselves up as 'developed mediums' and open their doors to people who want to part with their money and hopefully learn something, when in reality, they might as well have a good night out or follow some other pleasurable pursuit. At the time of writing this, circle leaders charge between one and 10 pounds sterling for a one and a half hour or two hour session. The choice of a competent medium should be taken with care, as not all who hold qualifications have the ability to teach—just as in any walk of life. The best choice is by recommendation. It should also be noted that there are many 'mediums' who have no qualifications at all!

This book is also intended as a sincere approach to the teaching of mediumship with some of the steps required to get there. The writer has been involved with 'Spiritualism' for well over 50 years, and has run development groups, worked in churches and centres, together with his wife, in England and abroad, taught and demonstrated healing; run open, closed and physical circles; has become a certificated medium, healer, counsellor and an ordained Minister.

For a long time I have been watching mediums that demonstrate and mediums that teach. As with any other area, the two aspects do not always go together. Much has been said, and has appeared in the press, about the quality of mediumship in the 21st century. It has not been complimentary! It really comes down to how each individual is taught and how they then develop themselves. If we are true to our calling, then we must continue to develop and learn properly. I put the generally low quality of mediumship to insufficient application to the job in hand by those who teach and those who learn, also the problem of wanting to have instantaneous ability without the proper application and dedication.

Once, at a psychic fair, I saw someone giving a reading for money using the Tarot, and reading the interpretation straight out of a book. If one considers the fine mediums of the past, such as Gordon Higginson and Albert Best, they were not content to sit back and say 'I know it all'. They continued to strive to improve what they had. There are mediums that are in the limelight today who need to increase the quality of what they do. All it takes is dedication to the betterment of quality, not—as a first consideration—how much money can I make? I do agree with being paid for what they do, but there is a limit.

This book is aimed at lifting the level of awareness and competency across the spectrum of psychic/spiritual work. To that end, the majority of information is slanted towards the teaching of students in the confines of a closed circle. One aspect that does not usually come across as an underlying premise is the use of the mind. This is the most fantastic tool that has ever been given to man. The problem with most people is that it's like playing with a very sophisticated computer, and they only know how to switch it on and off, and sometimes with a little bit of effort, try and make something work.

The mind is used in healing where a positive, although passive, thought is used to promote healing. The instances of success are quite staggering. If one then considers the venom and strength from an argument, does this not harm the recipient? It has been proved that by continually telling a child that they are either ugly or beautiful will make them actually take on that aspect.

I offer this book for your perusal, and hopefully your digestion. I am not in any way 'The Oracle' on all that can be taught about the realm of mediumship. The main reason in producing this book, is because so many people have asked me so many questions over the years that it seemed a good idea, especially in the light that, at present, there are no books covering the whole spectrum. So to those who aspire towards teaching, please be aware that you may instil in other people's minds something that you really ought not to do, if you are not very careful. Teaching, and especially in this context, needs careful thought before putting into operation. The phrase 'get the brain into gear before connecting the mouth' is a good analogy.

CHAPTER 1

BASIC UNDERSTANDING

To state the obvious, anyone who is in any way unstable of mind, who has real emotional problems or is an unstable character, should not become involved with anything that is in this book. Other than that, anyone with an open mind can benefit from spiritual teachings.

This is not an area to embark on if you wish to make lots of money. Indeed, there are very few 'good' mediums that earn an acceptable living. There should be a need to do this work that emanates from your very soul. The only way to view this is as a service to other human beings, who want, or need, a contact from the people who they knew before they left this earthly life or 'died'. Some have likened the work to counselling, and there are parallels.

The contents of this book is to help the true seeker to find their way through a myriad of false trails and difficult hurdles, but mainly for use as a reference book for the more advanced practitioner or teacher. You will not end up as a fantastic Tarot reader, nor will it help you to use any other divination methods because that is not what it is in this book. You will build on those aspects that you already have; common sense, awareness and the ability to use your mind. Within each of us there are many talents that we did not know we had until we tried to use them. How many of you accept that drawing and painting are inherent gifts that just need proper development? There is something more, much deeper inside of us that will not show until we try to use that facility.

To put it in a more up-to-date situation, just look at driving a car. In fact that is a very good analogy. We can learn what we are taught, but when we are allowed to spread our wings (passing the test), do we carry on with those teachings or do we decide that we now know better than anyone else and career along the road without a thought for other road users, or even improving our skills?

The mind is one of the most under-rated tools that we use. Consider the use of absent healing. We use our minds to ask our spirit friends to help make somebody better. This is the use of our mind and spirit mind for the betterment of others. Have you tried the following experiments?

On a day when there is sunshine and a few clouds, look at the clouds and using your mind make the clouds dissipate. Or—use your mind to communicate with an animal. If you are at a zoo, ask your selected animal to do something that is different to what is currently doing. For instance, if it is standing, use your mind to cause it lay down. Or—if you are nicely relaxed in your armchair at home, use your mind to get your partner to bring you a cup of tea. It is a fun occupation, but of course there are limits to what you should do. In the last example, you may get lumbered with the washing up!

Now consider the use of anger. We are not passive when angry, as we would be if we give healing. Additionally, when angry, and giving vent to our feelings, we use such vehemence that we must be doing a lot of harm to the person to whom we are directing it! When this aspect is considered, why should anyone be angry? The reason is either through frustration or because we think we know better than the other person. This not an aspect that is acceptable in any walk of life. I will admit, that to be at all times placid, is a great difficulty.

Using simple logic, we are all responsible for what we say and what we do. But all of this is initiated by our thoughts. Do we allow ourselves the time to seriously consider what we are going to say before we say it, and do we understand the repercussions? Usually not. If we are to become a spiritual person—and I do not think that the vast majority will ever make sainthood—we still need to do more as humans to make this world a better place to live in. Each of us has the ability to make changes, both in our own lives and others, by what we think, what we say and what we do.

Those of us who have entered our 'spiritual life on earth' realise that what we are doing is to live our religion, which is our way of life. Spiritualists do not go on an evangelical road because we have to find that spark within ourselves to want to make not only our own lives better, but to improve the lives of all on this earth. Some could say that we should be more 'Christian' because that used to be an ideal promoted by many in older times. The problem that I have with that is that so many wars have been fought in the name of Christianity, notably the Crusades and the Spanish Inquisition and various other factions, that it is now meaningless and has oppressed so many lives. Even now those who have the same general beliefs, with a small variation, are at war with each other. What a waste!

My own quest took a number of years to find the belief that suited *me*. That said—and I used the same words when I addressed a large gathering of secondary schoolchildren taken from all over Somerset—I am not here in this world asking you to believe that which I do. My belief came about through personal experiences and knowledge. If you wish to follow my pathway, then please be very aware what you are doing and the reasons why. Any belief must come from within, to satisfy you, the spiritual person, and not because somebody else said it was a good idea, or because your family said that that is what you must become. I hasten to add, that I do not want anyone to change their beliefs, unless they really and truly NEED to. Just be aware what it is that you believe in, and trust your own self to follow your best intentions for all the right reasons. At the same time, your beliefs should not to be forced upon others.

There are so many people who have allowed their beliefs to fade into disuse, for whatever reason. That is their choice. One wonders why? Maybe it is because those beliefs have not been nurtured due to the pressures of life. Where I live, in the South East of England, everybody is so caught up with a busy life, there seems to be little time to spend on other areas, such as our own spirituality and beliefs. When I visit people to arrange funerals, it is quite a catch up time and a re-assessment of what both the beliefs of the deceased and the funeral arranger's beliefs really are. It is a shame that a belief of whatever kind is put on the back shelf until it is nearly too late.

CHAPTER 2

THE PHILOSOPHY

INTRODUCTION

There seem to be a number of different avenues leading to seeking more information on Spiritualism. Obviously, a delving into world religions is one avenue, visiting a Spiritualist Church (or Centre) is another, a third is by going for a reading with a medium, and yet another can be by reading books written by contemporary mediums.

This seems to be a convenient point to introduce 'the Spiritualist', but before stating what a Spiritualist is, it seems more reasonable to state what a Spiritualist is not. He or she is not a dabbler in witchcraft, black or white magic; not someone who 'calls up the dead', not a fortune-teller and not a member of an illegal weird sect.

Spiritualism is a legally formed, recognised world religion. In the United Kingdom it is as acceptable as the Church of England or any other major religion. It is more than some religions, in that it is a way of life, not confined within the trappings of orthodoxy. The difference between a Spiritualist and any other normal, rational human being is that they believe that when a body dies, the spirit lives on. Not only does the spirit live on, but also that the intelligence and personality that was in the body can and does communicate with the living (and that means you and me!).

A Spiritualist, as with other religions, knows that words and actions are faculties that we should use with love, wisdom and moderation. I would like to ask all those who are considering getting more involved with becoming a medium, or even those who are just understanding what it is all about, to take their time and carefully dissect all the information that is obtained. A life-changing decision should only be taken with due care and consideration, and then to double check that this is the right course to take. My concern is that we should all do things for the right reasons, and a whim—or it seems a good idea at the time—is not the right reason.

Those who have been involved in spiritual work may wish to give this chapter only a cursory glance, but there are many who are totally unaware where they may be led, and are ignorant of some of the basic rules and the meanings of words that are used. It is necessary to start somewhere, and to start at the very beginning seems the logical place. There is a Glossary at the end of this book to explain the specific words used both in this book and by the workers who are spiritualists.

First of all, is the spirit world full of sweetness and light? The answer is a definite NO! Those of this world who do hateful things to others do not immediately become saints, just because they died. A biblical quotation explains this: *In my house there are many mansions.*

Although Spiritualism is an accepted religion, it is, more importantly, a way of life. It has a similarity to most other religions—including Christianity—by the concept that we should be nice to each other! If we all carried out our basic beliefs, then there would be no more wars. Problems arise when fanatics take one aspect of one religion and say that is the whole. It is prevalent in a number of different religions. These people are usually called fundamentalists. Wider reference is given in Chapter 21.

Spiritualism covers the following areas: hands-on healing; absent (or distant) healing; communication with those who have died and left this earthly world, this can be either directly through our own efforts or through the ability of a medium; and providing the ability for some mediums to channel someone from the spirit world for the purpose of giving philosophy and direct voice from a loved one; and also to allow, when the circumstances are ideal, for someone from the spirit world to materialise to speak directly with their loved ones and sometimes to be able to physically touch them. This provides so much more comfort than a priest or vicar saying that they have 'gone to a better place'!

There has been much said about Modern Spiritualism, but few talk about when the 'Old Spiritualism' started. It is my belief that was many years ago when Ancestor Worship was prevalent. It was at this time when it was natural for us humans to be able to discern the spirit bodies of our loved ones after their earthly death. If you read history over the years, you will understand that other beliefs negated these aspects, including the stupid accusations of witchcraft against mediums and spiritual persons. If a body of people disagree with something that they do not like, even today when we are supposed to be educated, then they will make a law to ban what they do not like.

Your first impression will be; should I then become involved? If you then ask yourself, would you like to seriously learn more, and you feel that you would, then please read on. Many people first get involved with the spiritual side of life through a number of different pathways. Often the Tarot is a first step, although strictly speaking, this is divination and not necessarily a good or even spiritual communication. Other ways of coming into contact may be either with a demonstration by a medium in a theatre, church or centre; or by going to a medium for a private sitting or watching an 'entertainment' programme on the television. This 'entertainment' tag has upset many a good medium, because it is our <u>belief</u>, not entertainment or a theatrical presentation. Another way is the use of an Ouija board. This is not to be recommended, as many problems may arise through 'playing' with it, **including great physical harm**. If you allowed a small child to play with matches, you would expect them to get burnt! The principle is exactly the same with spiritual work. It is surprising that there has not been a 'Health and Safety' bulletin issued.

Spiritualist churches and centres can provide an insight into Spiritualism, but the problem here, is that there are many and varied mediums. Some are brilliant, but are few and far between. Generally, average mediums can, at times, give good evidence that the spirit of a person who has 'died' has a continuation of life. Unfortunately, because the time usually taken to train a competent medium is very short, and their whole life is not dedicated to improvement, the quality varies enormously. Additionally, very few mediums are interested in furthering their knowledge and abilities once they start receiving money for their current skills.

Television has caused more problems for Spiritualism than that which is deserved. This is because it is advertised as 'entertainment'. Why are the Church of England and the Roman Catholic Church not advertised in the same way? Consider the 'top' mediums that demonstrate their way of life in large theatres and on television. Here, maybe up to about 5 to 10 people get a 'message' out of an audience of up to 3,000 or even more! The concept of living after we die is not a new idea. There are many people in this world who believe that there is an afterlife, but do not profess to be spiritualists.

Mediums that work quietly out of the public eye, who really want to improve their abilities on a day-to-day basis are often much better than the well-known ones. I have been fortunate to meet many such mediums, and their main worry is: *Am I doing a good enough job?* not, how much money can I make. Mediums should only be consulted by recommendation, and also, when there is a real need for a spiritual contact. As an aside, mediums are not doing their work when sorting out material problems (i.e. psychic work), although many add that aspect to their mediumistic abilities. A good medium will not only be mediumistic, but also have psychic and counselling skills. Not all are able to do this.

Reading autobiographies can be quite entertaining, but I have read a few by some mediums that have produced several books. Unfortunately, parts have been repeated in the next volume in the series. For the serious reader, there are many books that are inspiring, such as those by White Eagle. The Spiritualists that were living between 50 and 100 years ago have written much that is worth reading. I am not recommending any specific books for the reader to acquire, because there are so many, and also because we each have different needs, although, for reference, I have provided some information in Chapter 20.

CHAKRAS

An understanding of Chakras is also necessary. There are many books on the subject, so I will not go into a great deal of depth. It should be noted that some people do have a slightly different understanding and approach to others, but the principle remains the same.

There are seven main Chakras. Starting at the base of the spine (or Kundalini), the colour associated with it is red. The next, which is roughly two fingers width below the navel, is the sacral, with the colour orange. The sacral is used both in martial arts and breathing and is also known as the Tan Tien centre. Next is the solar plexus, two fingers width above the navel, with the colour yellow. Above that is the heart, (this is often depicted as being on the centre line of the body) with the colour green. These constitute the four lower Chakras.

The three upper Chakras are the throat, with the colour indigo; the centre of the forehead or third eye, with the colour mauve; and lastly the crown, which is on the top of the head, with the colour of either silver or gold, depending which teaching is followed.

These are the main Chakras. There are more. For instance the hands and feet contain Chakras, but are less publicised than the main ones. We use the hand Chakras for healing.

Each main Chakra needs to have some sort of closure after use. This is for protection. In the initial stages of development, it is essential to use these Chakras properly. I allow my students to visualise their own form of closure. This could be a heavy wooden door with bolts, a porthole with clamps, or anything else that incorporates something that opens and closes and additionally has a means of locking. The dual system is so that the mind acknowledges the positivity of the action, and by using the mind in this way, actual protection is attained.

When starting to work with spirit AND when under the control of a competent circle leader, the Chakras are opened properly. The chakras will open automatically when working in a spiritual sense, but if opened properly they will work much better. When work with spirit has been completed, the Chakras must be closed properly. It is worth noting, that the closure at the end of a session is good, but if talk then returns to spiritual work, then the Chakras will automatically re-open. Therefore I teach that when the circle has finished and the students are away from each other (maybe sitting in their car before they start it, to go home) that is the time to close down. Normal convention is that we open UP and close DOWN, although for some unknown reason, others use the opposite direction.

Why am I involved in this way of life? It is because I think that we can be of benefit to each other to enable our lives to be more complete. Over the ages there has always been a need for some sort of belief, even if it is only believing in ourselves. There is also a need for hope, and this spiritual way can provide it. Most people at some stage in their life will begin to think about their own mortality. The next thought can be terrifying. Where am I going, or, is this it, it's all over; or, what are those that I am leaving, going to do without me? The other side of the coin is; what am I going to do when my parents or lover has died?

This way of life is based on the belief that we all go to the spirit world. All of us, regardless of whether or not we are good people will go there. Those that are murderers, paedophiles and suicides all go to the spirit world, although not to the same area (thank goodness!). By the way, suicides are not condemned by the spirit world, even if it is against the law in some countries. We will have the opportunity to meet our loved ones again. This is based on the evidence that is provided by mediums. Regardless of those that sneer and argue against our belief, there is overwhelming evidence that there is a spirit world. It is quite funny, that when non-believers get to the spirit world, how they have to change their mind.

If we have a strong bond with someone, then we shall be with that person in the spirit world. If we have had a general relationship with someone, maybe a relative who was not close, we can still have contact with them in the spirit world, if we both wish.

I believe that when we go to the spirit world, if we are a particularly nasty sort of person that we go to somewhere different from where the 'nice' people are. There is a saying in the spiritualist's vocabulary, which is as relevant with regard to our spirit friends, as in this earthly world; *like attracts like*. This also implies that those that we are not similar to, we do not come into contact with. If there is a need, then this can be overridden for a short time.

CHAPTER 3

THE CIRCLE LEADER

It is widely assumed that any practicing medium can teach. This not so. As with any other profession, a teacher needs to know more than how to do the job that they do.

I have seen many so-called mediums who 'teach' mediumship. Most try to make clones of themselves, many just have a stab at it and expect their pupils to become fantastic mediums—but certainly NOT as good as the leader, as it may take away their livelihood! Others just do not have a clue. Both my wife and I have always taken great care to ensure that those who we teach are not just as good as us, but far better.

Just going through the motions does not teach. Each person is an individual, and therefore must be taught according to each person's ability, and to try and make them the best medium that they can ever be. This takes time and dedication on the part of the pupil and the leader.

I have seen leaders who give a lesson and sit back and wait for the pupils to shine. It is not surprising that they do not shine, mainly because of the lack of effort from the leader—and sometimes through lack of interest. It is a well-known fact that some leaders only teach for the money—not for the benefit of the pupils.

With groups that I have taken, I know what each and every pupil has experienced when they are asked to provide mediumship. I link in with them. It is quite humorous when they forget some of what they have envisaged, and I prompt them as to what they forgot.

There are some mediums who are in the public eye who have many clones of themselves, this includes how they use their hands, their stance, little asides that are nothing to do with mediumship, and so on.

The correct way to teach is to show the pupil a way of doing a particular aspect of mediumship and see how they get on. If they find it difficult, then approach the same aspect from a different perspective, and keep on changing that approach until they find the best way of working for that pupil. By doing this, each pupil will then have a number of ways in which to achieve the desired results.

For the pupil, you need to ensure that the person who is teaching, really does know what they are doing, and that you will learn not only about how to provide good mediumship, but all the intricacies of how it is done.

The above words may give you the feeling that I am biased against circle leaders. I am not really, but the quality of mediumship over the last 20 to 30 years has deteriorated to such an extent that it often does not bear any comparison to the 'great' mediums of the past. Many mediums seem to think that a psychic connection is all that is needed, and that real communication with the spirit world is not always needed.

This—in part—is caused by bad circle leaders. The other part is caused by how life is led at this time. Mostly it is 'I have a problem, please sort it out, as I do not know how'. This is not a mediumship problem. It is more to do with counseling. Mediumship, in its purest form, can give grieving families and friends a sense of hope and acceptance, which psychic information cannot.

The circle leader is the one person to whom a lot of responsibility is given. Apart from training, which is a big enough job, the responsibility of ensuring that mediumship is taught at a high level of quality and that the continuation of that quality is also maintained. It is a very responsible job. At its best the circle leader will improve the quality of mediumship with all that they meet. There is only one problem, and that is the leader must be able to demonstrate their mediumship at the highest quality. This is not always easy to achieve, and with some they will never achieve it. Those are the ones who should never teach.

With each type of circle there is a different type of approach and therefore the circle leader often cannot lead each type. The types of circles that need differing approaches are: Open, Closed, Healing, Trance and Physical.

The Open Circle needs a leader who can cope with possession, drama queens and those with a vivid sense of imagination. The last two require common sense, although it is sometimes difficult to clearly define who is being true to what they are doing, and those who believe that what they are doing is true. I have had occasion, when running an open circle, to immediately close it when two girls showed clear signs of unwanted spirits interfering with their normal behaviour. It became both distressing for the girls and also the rest of the sitters. The ability to clear unwanted spirits is paramount, as is the common sense.

The Closed Circle needs a leader who can and does link in with each sitter. It is no good just giving exercises that have been learnt, and then hope that the sitters can then become mediums. I have seen too many so-called mediums running a circle, and they have not any idea as to what they are supposed to be doing. In closed circles that I have taken, I know what each sitter gets. If the leader cannot do that then they should not be running a circle. Some leaders also think that a closed circle is OK to have different people sitting. That is an open circle. A closed circle means just that. Closed. No changes to the sitters.

A Healing Circle needs a leader who is obviously a healer, but a healer with a lot of experience. It has been known for patients to go into trance when receiving healing, and in a rare case, a patient lost control of their bodily functions when in an altered state. Again, the leader needs to know more than just a superficial amount about contact with the guides.

A Trance Circle needs a leader who is well versed in control of spirit guides and the parameters of that control. It needs someone who is both a strong medium and who also has a good degree of sensitivity. There is a need to be able to be confident enough to control people in whatever situation presents itself. Spirit guides are people who live in the spirit world. They have the same mannerisms as they did when on earth. This means that sometimes leaders have to be a little bit democratic in what they say and do.

A Physical Circle needs a leader who requires the attributes of a Trance Circle leader, and also have extra skills, such as being able to operate in the dark or low light situations. Before a sitting the leader is responsible for setting out the rules of the sitting and being strong enough to bar entry to anyone who may not respect the precepts of the sitting. The leader controls what is, and is not taken into the séance room and is responsible for the discipline within the séance room. There has been an occasion where I have had to close a circle because a circle member did something that I specifically asked them not to, which was trying to grab the ectoplasm. The medium suffered a blow to the stomach when the ectoplasm went back into his body. The sitter (who was a friend) lost both the ability to sit again and also our friendship. The other sitters lost the rest of that evening.

Chapter 4

PREPARATION

It is very difficult (and maybe impossible) for the majority of people to sit down and ensure that there are no residual worries or problems in the mind. To do any spiritual work there needs to be calmness, clearness of mind and a relaxed state of both mind and body. Without these parameters, which should be present prior to each time work is done; there will be no appreciable progress. Many people who sit in a chair cannot relax. Others may have been doing physical work and cannot relax. Do not despair! Help is at hand. Many years ago I was the Regional Pistol Coach for the Southeast of England, and part of my job was to take a class of about 50 people who had just been involved with quite strenuous physical exercise, and bring them to a relaxed state and also to reduce their pulse beat.

The following is the exercise that I devised. In the group of 50 people, two or three would go to sleep—so I know that it works. This series of exercises may take a little while to soak up, but they can be aided by a friend recording an audio tape for you.

1. Sit in an upright chair with your feet placed firmly on the floor, arms in your lap and your head erect.

2. Breathe in through the nose consciously, pulling the stomach in and expanding the chest. Breathe out through the mouth. Repeat twice. Be aware of all movement of air.

3. Straighten the legs, ensuring that the heels remain on the floor.

4. Push the toes away, keeping the heels on the floor, and then relax. Repeat twice.

5. Pull the toes towards you, keeping the heels on the floor, and then relax. Repeat twice.

6. Replace your feet firmly on the floor.

7. Put your hands on the outside of your knees with the palms facing in. Push outwards with your knees and inwards with your hands, and then relax. There should be no apparent movement, but make all the muscles in those areas work. Repeat twice.

8. Put your hands on the inside of your knees with the palms facing out (it might be easier to swap the hands over). Reverse the pressures and then relax. Repeat twice.

9. Repeat step 1.

10. Try and push your bottom into the corner between the back and seat. Feel the stomach and chest muscles work, and then relax. Repeat twice.

11. Allow your arms to hang down by your sides. There are two exercises at the same time. Stretch the hands and fingers wide apart and push down with the shoulders, and then relax. Feel the muscles work. Repeat twice.

12. Position the hands, elbows and shoulders in one horizontal line. Move the elbows forward in six small circles, and then stop. Move the elbows backwards in six large circles, and then stop. Relax.

13. Interlace your fingers of both hands at the nape of your neck. Stretch, and then relax. Repeat twice.

14. Allow your hands to hang down by your sides. Stretch your neck upwards, and then relax. Repeat twice.

15. Stifle a yawn. Repeat twice.

16. Push your tongue down into the lower jaw. Repeat twice.

17. Close your eyes. Place the tips of your fingers of both hands together, in the centre of your forehead. Relax the hands so that your hands *just* touch your forehead around to the ears. Very, very slowly, keeping the fingers still touching, and with a feather light touch, move both hands to the rear of the head and down to the nape of the neck. Be very aware of the feelings on the head (i.e. hair movement and scalp reaction). Repeat twice.

18. Repeat step 1.

19. Recreate the feelings encountered in step 17. Repeat twice. If unable to re-create the feelings, repeat step 17.

20. Become aware of breathing. Feel the breath moving up through the nostrils, down the throat and into the lungs, then exhale through the mouth, still aware of the breath.

21. Very gently pause both at the inhaled and exhaled states. Breathe in this manner for a short while.

22. Visualise a scene that is both quiescent and calming. Relax.

This series of exercises may take a little while to soak up, but remember, they can be aided by a friend recording a tape for you. It is well known that many people do not like the sound of their own voice in this situation, and someone with a calm and well-modulated voice can really enhance these exercises. It will take a bit of practice, but if you persevere, you will achieve a changed state.

I suggest that Chapter 6 should also be read, as breathing is a very important part to your preparation. Other aspects within the parameters of preparation is cleanliness, using the same clothes (after being washed), being relaxed and placid in mind, not rushing about, taking time before doing any spiritual work to sit down with a piece of relaxing music playing and become harmonious with all that is around you.

Most people that I know, even the mediumistic ones, often do not really prepare themselves. Generally, preparation to most people is sitting down and getting their breath back, trying to relax their mind ready for whatever comes. With many, they do not see the need for preparation, but over the years, I have realised that without good preparation, things can go wrong. I have to say that my wife takes about 15 to 30 minutes to link with the spirit world as part of her preparation, before giving a sitting.

In an ideal world, we would all be worry-free, relaxed, full of energy and mentally alert. As this is not usually the case, we have to devise some way of offsetting that which we do have. Worry-free is an attitude of mind that we can control, even though it may be difficult. The only way that I know how to stop worrying about anything is to concentrate on something else. Before you reject this thought, let me provide a piece of information. If you have a drippy nose, and then become totally immersed in doing some sort of activity, the drip seems to stop. It is exactly the same principle in a mediumistic sense. When I was on parade, whilst in the Royal Air Force, we were taught to counteract an irritation (wherever it might be), by imagining the irritation as a pressure. This does work.

If we really concentrate on our breathing or follow a meditation, other thoughts will tend to fade. Relaxation can also be achieved by carrying out the above relaxation technique. Energy can be obtained by reading Chapter 7 and following the suggestions. To be mentally alert is a little more difficult. Brain tiredness can really only be treated with sleep, therefore, when there is the need for preparation, the planning must start earlier, by going to bed at a reasonable time and having sufficient sleep to recharge the batteries. We each have sufficient information within ourselves, but it seems that there are times when we forget that to function properly; we need to undertake certain maintenance procedures on our bodies and minds.

Preparation also means to condition, over a period of time, the way we think and the way we see ourselves. There is a need to ensure that we do things for the right reasons. There is a need to understand what makes other people tick. Consider how you would feel if you went to see a medium that was off-hand with you, did not respect you and maybe showed some anger towards you. Would you feel happy about getting a message from your loved one? We need to speak to those true friends that we have to get some honest feedback as to our personality and general demeanour. We could then change so that which is projected by our personality becomes attractive. This would help enormously with our new selves being a medium. Although it is accepted that nobody can force us to change, we can, if we want to, change ourselves.

Another way of being prepared is to look at the presentation of ourselves. This is how we are perceived in the manner of our dress or the way in which we speak and move. Our clothing does not have to be anything other than clean and smart, depending on the place that we will be. Our language needs to have some control, without even any mild blasphemies. We need to speak clearly with sufficient power to reach all the people that are being spoken to, without shouting. The quality level of speech should be at the mid-standard of the majority, with no patronising or other demeaning effects.

If other people feel comfortable in your company and trust you implicitly, then you have probably got it right, but if the opposite is true, then there is only one person that the blame can rest with, and that is you. If this is unfortunately the case, then a good friend can help you a lot by providing you with honest information. As this is a multi-facetted possibility, you would have to work out what to do to put everything right, but again, your friends could help.

OPENING UP

Opening up is the first step to being ready for spirit communication. Assuming that you have read about Chakras, we can then move on to making them work.

1. When the preparation is complete, first of all imagine that, with the feet flat on the floor, a copper rod extends from your heel into the earth below.

2. Next, visualise your base Chakra (together with its colour if you wish) as a door, which is locked. Visualise the unlocking of the door and then open the door wide.

3. Continue in this way through the other six Chakras.

4. On the last Chakra, add the following: Imagine a golden light that leaves the top of your head and stretches all the way to the spirit world.

CLOSING DOWN

1. Start at the top of the head and visualise the golden light withdrawing back into your crown.

2. When that is done, imagine closing the door to the Chakra and locking it.

3. Continue in this way through the other six Chakras.

4. When you have completed the last Chakra, visualise a blue light completely enclosing you, so as to provide extra protection.

There are variations to the above, dependant on how each individual feels. Some may, instead of using a door, like to use a flower opening and closing or even some other means. The main achievement is to have a means of opening and closing, but with the added part of ensuring an extra 'lock'. Some may like to use a ribbon or padlock and chain. At the end of the day it is what feels most right for each individual.

Closing down can be very useful when outside of the 'spiritual' context. For instance, I was working in the Netherlands, in charge of a large technical publications department, when I felt 'peculiar'. After a few minutes, I realised that I was picking up negative thoughts that were pushed in my direction by someone who thought that they should be doing my job instead of me. I 'closed down', and the feeling passed. It is a means of self-protection that should not be ignored, and can be used in other situations apart from spiritual ones.

There are some mediums who 'close down' as soon as they wake up in the morning, because they will automatically 'open up' while asleep. Closing down at the end of a circle is good practice and as time goes by, one can 'open up' and 'close down' in a few seconds.

A point to remember is that within a circle, after 'closing down', if talk continues about spirit in general, the automatic aspect of 'opening up' happens. Therefore, when away from discussions with others about what happened in circle, again, 'close down'. This is not about playing at spirit contact, but keeping yourself safe.

There is a very distinct difference between unconsciously 'opening up' and going through a set exercise of 'opening up'. The exercise always works better. Hoping that you are 'closed down' does not work. Always 'close down in a structured way, it is better to be safe than sorry!

CHAPTER 5

CIRCLES

Dealing with clairvoyance and its development, there are two types of circle; open and closed. There are also healing and physical circles, which can include trance in both cases.

There is a great need for competent circle leaders, because there are so many people who wish to learn and understand this multi-facetted subject. The leaders are not teachers in the accepted sense, because each novice can, and often does, develop differently from the leader, also the leader often learns from the pupils. The leader provides the base from which to develop, and guides the novices through different techniques. This determines the best way for that individual to work. An ideal leader will provide many different techniques for each pupil, to ensure that each pupil is provided with the best techniques so that they can develop to the best ability that they can. In an ideal world, no person should have mediocre information to restrict their potential, although in the real world, there are mediums/circle leaders who do not wish their pupils to do as well as they, because it would be taking work (and potentially money) away from the leader. Both my wife and I adhere to the precept that we are willing to impart all the information and techniques that we have, and hope (and expect) that our pupils will exceed our abilities.

Open Circle

An open circle is where the ability to sit together for development is open to anyone. It could be viewed as a taster to sitting in a closed circle. There is usually a lower age limit, because at this time, for a child to sit in any sort of circle is assumed to be dangerous. Personally, I would bar all children under 18 from sitting in an open circle, but would be quite happy for a child, who is fit in mind and body, and a teenager, to sit in a closed circle, provided the parent, or guardian, gives permission. It would seem prudent before initiating the open circle to have a question answered by all who wish to sit, and that is: 'Why do you want to sit in this circle?'. The answers may give some insight to the leader as to the stability and aspirations of each sitter.

I have seen open circles that contain over 30 people in it. It becomes unwieldy with too many people, so common sense must dictate the limit of numbers. Sometimes the general aspects of the room are not considered, such as lighting level and external noise. Obviously the circle leader needs to **really** control the events. A high degree of discipline is essential, because indiscriminate chatting will waste time and can destroy relaxed concentration. The chairs are placed in a circle so that the leader can see everyone; hence the term 'circle' is used.

When considering sitting in a circle, the circle leader needs to be looked at from two viewpoints. The first is, has this person the ability, sensitivity and knowledge to conduct the circle, and the second is from the sitters' point of view, do I feel safe?

Taking the aspect of ability, it would be prudent to say that the requirements should include both the ability to demonstrate that which is being taught, and also to have the ability to provide information in a way and at a level for the sitters to understand.
Sensitivity to all sitters is required because with the wrong words or attitude, even if only one of the sitters may be deeply offended, the others will also pick up on that fact, which could alienate all.

An additional aspect is the requirement to be able to deal with anything that may arise, including possession, trance—and with some people the ability to discern the difference between fact and fallacy. For instance; there are some people who think that they are in trance and the perception may be that this is correct, but it can either be an act, or lack of control of imagination. Leaders need to know the difference and be strong enough to tell the individual that has a strong imagination what they are doing wrong, and also in a manner that is not aggressive.

The purpose of the circle should be explained carefully and each time it is formed, as the persons attending may not be the same. The circle may be for meditation and visualisation, to quiet the mind and body and to be aware of the use of the mind's (third) eye. In this case, a relaxation exercise may be given in which the limbs and body are brought to a relaxed state. Next, I recommend that the Egyptian meditation position should be taken. This is with a fairly straight back, head erect, feet flat on the floor and the hands loosely resting in the lap. Normally, after the parameters have been established, the leader opens the circle with a prayer asking for protection. When the circle has ended, the leader closes with a prayer of thanks. The leader has great responsibility because he/she controls everything that happens and is responsible for the spiritual and physical security of everyone there. It should be noted that trance is not permitted in an open circle because it can cause upset with other sitters—usually because they are not in the frame of mind to cope with it, or because the results could disrupt the circle.

A visualisation may be a rose, where the leader may suggest a colour and encourage the participants to also visualise the stem and leaf. This could be followed by visualising the rose opening and closing; from bud to fully open. Additionally, the leader may suggest being aware of a fragrance from the rose. All this stimulates the would-be medium to be aware of their senses and how to use them, just as an experienced medium would do.

Open circles can be hazardous for the person taking the circle (circle leader), and also the sitters. Because anyone can sit, there is no control of the possibility that unwelcome spirits could join and disrupt the circle. There have been occasions where sitters have been scared, due to mischievous spirits, and the only action that can be taken is for the circle leader to immediately close the circle. Based on my personal experience, as soon as the circle has been closed, the majority of people must leave the area. Those left behind should be only the circle leader and those who are affected by the disruption, so that the circle leader can deal with whatever happened.

There are various ways of cleansing the people and the room. One way is to provide healing for those concerned, but if the situation is worse, then it may be necessary to carry out an exorcism. This then is the reason for a circle leader to be competent, with the full understanding of their responsibility and also to be able to cope with any emergency. It is not sufficient for the circle leader to know a little bit and hope that it all works out. This is an area where practical knowledge is essential—but not only knowledge; it also needs capability to deal with any eventuality; from just being scared to being taken over by an unwelcome spirit.

People who are searching should only sit in an open circle for a few times, because they will then find out whether this line of development is right for them. If it is, then they need to find a closed circle that is run by a person who is competent. The assumption should not be made, that any medium would be competent, either for an open circle or a closed one. Circle leaders should be questioned as to their experience and competence, by asking the leader directly and also others who know the leader. There have been a number of people who have been possessed, and the resultant work to stabilise the situation, that has been required is often difficult and upsetting. It can be seen that novices should be very careful with whom they sit. Sometimes there have been some wonderful happenings even with a leader who is not very competent. My wife first met her main guide in an open circle, but this was a bit unusual because she had been spiritually ready to work with spirit, but kept putting it off. Six weeks later she was working on platform—again, unusual.

The circle leader, if they are good, will be vigilant. This is to ensure that no harm comes to any of the sitters and to watch what is happening in their development. The amount of time sitting in an open circle should not be long. First of all the leader should explain what is required from each person and what may happen, describing all aspects so that fear will be at a minimum. Those areas are: feelings, being touched, visions of colour, awareness that someone may be close to them, when in fact nobody (physical) is there, sensations of 'not being in control', etcetera.

Another purpose of an open circle could be to open a link with spirit communication. The relaxation exercise, as previously mentioned, may be the start. The use of music can be helpful to relax the mind, but the selection must be careful because what might suit one person may not suit another. Having talked about the five senses, (being aware of actual touch, sight, hearing, tasting and smell—and also 'feeling' the same 5 senses—plus 'sixth' sense and the ability to 'see' 3 ways—actual, visualisation and seeing spirit), the leader may then request those who are taking part to have an 'open' mind, be aware of the senses and then wait for spirit communication. The leader may then give further information, so that the participants can deduce who the communication (or message) is for. In many cases the message may be for the person sitting directly opposite the one who received the communication. Alternatively, an impression of a face or a name, or even a 'pull' to one side can identify the recipient. A quiet time is necessary, the leader having stated that after a few minutes (usually six or seven) the group would be gently brought back to reality. Nothing is worse than for someone sitting in a circle not knowing what to expect and how long to keep their eyes closed.

Each member of the group is asked for their reactions; what impressions they had received and who they thought the message was for. This is done in an indiscriminate way, rather than going around the circle, so that all of the group pay attention to the proceedings. The leader elicits all relevant information and helps with the interpretation. Often it is easier to get information than to know how to interpret it.

CLOSED CIRCLE

I am repeating the introduction to the open circle as some who are reading this as a reference book may skip that part. It is just as important for all types of circle. The circle leader needs to be looked at from two viewpoints. The first is has this person the ability to conduct the circle, and the second is from the sitters' point of view, do I feel safe?

Taking the aspect of ability, it would be prudent to say that the requirements should include both the ability to demonstrate that which is being taught, and also to have the ability to provide information in a way and at a level for the sitters to understand. Sensitivity to all sitters is required because with the wrong words or attitude, even if only one of the sitters may be deeply offended, the others will also pick up on that fact, which could alienate all. An additional aspect is the requirement to be able to deal with anything that may arise, including possession, trance—and with some people the ability to discern the difference between fact and fallacy. For instance; there are some people who think that they are in trance and the perception may be that this is correct, but it can either be an act, or lack of control of imagination.

Before accepting a person to sit in a closed circle, the leader should have an informal chat with the applicant to ascertain the level of development, together with attitudes to spirituality (not spiritualism) and personality. These aspects can make a large difference when trying to blend all circle members. Having decided on who should comprise the circle (often 5 to 9 sitters, plus the leader), the next step is to decide where the circle members will sit in relation to each other. This is to balance the energies. Usually, the leader, together with those conducting the circle from the spirit world will decide. It may be that some circle leaders will use a pendulum to check the energies. All the chairs in the circle should be of the upright type, to aid concentration, as a sloppy settee can invite a sloppy attitude, which could lead to indifference to what is happening. Each member of the circle should be provided with a glass of water, and in some instances a jug of water may be needed. Just a word of caution. Drinking too much water may necessitate visiting the toilet. In a circle, it is normal not to leave until the time together has finished. It is also worth-while, from the leader's control that the toilet should be made use of prior to commencement of the circle.

Although rarely done, it makes sense to have all the members meet together to have an informal chat to see how everyone gets on before commencing the circle. Any closed circle should be run on fairly strict lines. In this day and age, people generally like to do as they wish at any time. Because of this it is usual to state that permission has to be sought from the leader to miss a meeting, and if too many are missed, then the person will be asked to leave permanently. It is not unusual to allow non-attendance with holidays spent away from home, illness or other reason that cannot be accommodated. If sitters just decide that they cannot be bothered, then they are best dropped. It needs stable energies to run a good circle, and everyone is important to keep it stabilised. It is best to have about a weeks gap before really starting, as that means each would-be sitter can speak to the leader on an informal basis. This ensures that there will not be any surprises when the first sitting commences. At the informal meeting, dates and timings should be established to ensure that other commitments do not clash.

A room in which a circle is going to be held should be clean and tidy with sufficient seating, which should comprise chairs that are upright. Settees do not really work. Ventilation is often a necessity and it is useful to have small tables to put a glass of water on. If the room is to be used for other spiritual work, then please refer to Chapter 15 for the best parameters.

On the first sitting, and also all subsequent sittings, the circle is formed with the chairs, and the lighting is subdued. The sitters should be at the place where the meeting is about 10 to 15 minutes before the start time. They should be on their respective seats about 5 minutes before starting, and prepare themselves by relaxing. The leader could have some appropriate music playing. Then all the sitters should be encouraged to forget the daily/weekly problems and become serene in mind and body. At the start time the leader should open with a prayer and ask for a cloak of protection for the circle. Discipline is a necessity, therefore establishment of times and procedures should be paramount.

The leader should explain what the ensuing time would comprise. The first time that the group sit together is as a trial. Therefore the evening will be assessed by the leader, looking at the compatibility and suitability of everyone there. A trial period may be initiated of maybe six weeks (on a weekly basis). Each circle needs to run for a set time.

Usually a two-hour session is about right. Outside commitments are usually a problem, so definite parameters are necessary.

The closed circle can use the aspects used in the open circle, as described above. Most leaders state that there are the five senses that we use (smell, taste, touch, sight and hearing). I have modified them, so that the five senses have a greater number of possibilities for communication. Added to the five senses are 'I think', for instance: 'I think I hear'. The total is then 10 senses. There is also a 'sixth' sense of someone standing close, but unseen. The sense of sight is threefold, not two. One is normal vision, the second is visualisation and the third is actually seeing spirit as a solid person. This makes 12 senses, and spirit communication may come via any one, and may even be two or more senses at the same time.

Closed circles are formed with a specific objective in mind. The objective could be for the development of speakers or demonstrators who would work in churches. The circle could be for healing, trance, physical phenomena or general development. Additional works that can be included are psychometry, sand readings, inspirational writing and psychic drawing. Part of development is to get over shyness or ego in front of others and to be able to speak clearly.

As with an open circle, an experienced medium must control and lead the circle. It must be stressed that direction, control and discipline are necessary, as indifferent development does not give the budding medium the guidance required, but tends to confuse and distract from the proper objective.

A suggested way of running a weekly circle to develop novices for working in a church could be as follows, based on a four weekly cycle. This is basic information which will be explained in more depth where you see the*.

Week 1

After the basics, as mentioned above, the first part of the session is a reading of a short passage from either a poem or a spiritually inclined book, followed by an address or inspirational talk. This relates to the normal reading and address given in churches. The inspiration may be just by sensing, but in its purer form will be spoken through the person inspired, without their thinking mechanism being used. I have often objectively listened to what my inspirers are saying through my mouth. The second part is where each person stands with their face to a wall or corner of a room, then relates on how they feel or sense. The reason for facing the wall is to negate the use of the psychic abilities and to depend purely on the spirit communication.

WEEK 2

This is used to introduce other ways of picking up information, such as the use of psychometry, sand readings or mediumship, as specified by the leader. Automatic writing and inspirational drawings may also be attempted—but not at the same meeting!

WEEK 3

This can be in the form of a service. Each circle member prepares a reading and an address prior to the meeting. Each, in turn, presents the reading from a table (to provide a feeling of a church situation) in front of the others. After that each member returns to the table and gives two spirit inspired messages.

WEEK 4

Commencing with music in the background, the leader talks the group through a meditation. Visualisation and awareness of the senses is often the theme. A short discussion on the ethics and practicalities of healing can follow. After that contact healing is carried out under the guidance of the leader.

The aim is to give guidance, over a number of weeks or months, or even years, to eventually become a competent medium, speaker or healer and become an asset to the church.

*The above information is given as a guide only. Each week, 1, 2, 3 or 4, are started at an easy level, and ensuing meetings of each week can then be more involved, so that eventually, although the general parameters of the week remain the same, the depth will become greater as the months progress. When complete novices begin, they need to be taken gently through each step, ensuring that each aspect is clearly understood. Facing a wall is not as a punishment, but as an aid to having a clear mind with no distractions. The understanding of how a circle member can feel when absorbing impressions from a guide or communicator is greatly enhanced in this mode. Each leader gives information in different ways, and the purpose of this book is not to push any leader to do something different to that which they normally do.

Variation in the work that is done in a circle is necessary otherwise boredom creeps in, which could destroy the circle. Another type of closed circle is where all aspects of mediumship are taught, except physical. As long as the meetings are varied, much can be achieved. The subjects include: guided meditation, sensing, drawing, using psychic abilities, psychometry and mediumship. Additionally homework may be given to coax the circle member to communicate with their own guides, through inspirational writing. Often a single word is given, such as: love, hate, family, healing and colours. It is amazing what a variety of views can be witnessed. The homework is usually dealt with after the opening prayer and a meditation. We have kept the best inspirational information obtained from our students' circles—often given by spirit in a poetic form—and made an basic, home produced, book from them.

Physical mediumship and to a certain extent, trance and transfiguration are separate circles. There are people who wish to join a circle, but mention anything out of their normal concept and their perceived abilities, and there can be a feeling that physical spiritual development is a step too far.

To become a physical medium one needs to sit with a group of people who are totally dedicated to help just the medium, and also expect nothing in return for themselves. Obviously when the medium can be 'taken over' by spirit, they will have a ringside seat. I have been a circle leader for an excellent physical medium for a couple of years or so. During that time wonderful things have happened. This is more fully described in Chapter 15.

With trance and transfiguration, this could be incorporated within a normal development circle, but some may not wish to take part. Therefore a separate circle may be appropriate for that aspect of mediumship. I have included this type of development also in Chapter 15.

Various means are used to help people make a better link or communication. I have listed these under the following heading of Exercises.

EXERCISE 1: SENSING YOUR GUIDE

If you wish, have some pleasant, non-intrusive music playing. Sit in the Egyptian meditation position. Be aware of your surroundings, who is sitting next to you and what is around you. Be aware of a presence at your right hand shoulder and allow that feeling to grow. Ask for a touch, a perfume or a sound so that you will be able to recognise the same entity that is with you.

Note: the leader could put a hand on the right shoulder momentarily to aid concentration.

Once some form of communication has been established, ask for some basic information, such as male or female, tall or short, fat or thin. Continue in the same vein to build a mental picture of the guide or friend. Over a period of time a mental picture will build up.

EXERCISE 2: SENSING A COMMUNICATOR

This is similar to exercise 1, except the start is to stand up facing a corner of the room. The leader needs to help the pupil to sense the person who wishes to communicate with a person in the group or circle. Prompts should be used, such as: male/female, tall/short, fat/thin, hair colour, beard (males only), old/young, etcetera. Once the description has been established with another person in the room, then the pupil should turn around and carry on with the message.

EXERCISE 3: SENSING COLOURS (1)

There are many variations to this exercise, but the simplest one is where the pupil under tuition is blindfolded. We use about half a metre of different coloured materials, and let the pupil touch the material and state the colour. After some time of using this exercise, the pupils become quite adept. The practical purpose is to identify colours of clothes on a communicant, without actually seeing it.

EXERCISE 4: SENSING COLOURS (2)

The circle should have settled and each member is asked to close their eyes. Spend two minutes 'sending' a colour clockwise around the circle. The object is to feel the colour that is sent from the person on the right. The colour that is 'sent' may not be the colour that is received. This can be attempted a number of times with different colours and direction.

EXERCISE 5: WORKING WITH DIFFERENT SENSES

Earlier in this chapter I have said that I prefer to say that we have 12 senses. Because many people initially feel that they cannot work with that amount, I have devised an exercise so that when communication comes in on different senses, they can cope better. This is the exercise.

Sitting in a circle with eyes shut, imagine a colour of red. Imagine the colour going around the circle in a clockwise manner. Leave about one minute and then add the next colour (going up the chakras) of orange. Add the following colours at intervals, in order: yellow, green, indigo and mauve. Six colours only are used. This equates to using six senses.

The next dimension is to keep the colours going around, and then starting with the red, make it go around slowly. Make the orange go a little faster, and so on with the other colours. Eventually all the colours are rotating and each are at a different speed. This now equates to working with the 12 senses. By practising this exercise, mediums can pick up communication from different aspects much more easily.

EXERCISE 6: SORTING NUMBERS OF COMMUNICATORS

Place a chair in the corner of the room, facing the corner. Each pupil sits in the chair for each personal exercise. They are blindfolded. The leader then stands behind the pupil with their hands on the pupil's shoulders. The leader then says; you can feel me standing behind you. I am taking my hands away. Can you still sense me? The answer is usually 'yes'. The leader moves away and substitutes another person. This is done very quietly so that the pupil does not guess who is standing behind.

The pupil has to sense whether it is a male or female person standing behind them. When that is correct, the actual person should be identified. Once the rest of the group/circle has carried this out, the next part of the exercise starts. Exactly the same format is started, except that more than one person is standing behind the pupil. The pupil has to identify not only how many people are behind, but also what gender they are. If that is done well, then they could identify each person standing behind. I do not normally go above four people standing behind.

The only problem with this exercise is noise. When people move, there is some noise generated and it is not difficult to identify from which direction it comes. Using memory of where people are sitting, logic can dictate who is where. To overcome this, all participants should make a noise simultaneously, masking the person who actually moves.

CHAPTER 6

BREATHING

This is an area that has not had the amount of application that is necessary for proper spiritual work to be achieved. Breathing can make the difference between a mediocre demonstration of mediumship and an excellent one. There are two or three types of breathing, depending upon which school of thought one uses. Normal breathing should be when, with each breath, the rib cage moves. The second is where one breathes from the stomach. The third is where the shoulders are hunched up and the amount of air entering the lungs is minimal, it is often seen with people who have respiratory disease. A Yogic breath uses all three types.

Each individual reacts differently, so it is important to give sufficient time to practice to really ensure that each person can achieve their best potential. There are many ways of improving breathing, including yoga, Chi Kung and Tai Chi Ch'uan, and of course, breathing exercises. Generally, breathing frequency is at least 20 breaths each minute, but many advise an optimum of 6 to 8 breaths to enable our lungs to work better.

Because breathing is a natural phenomenon and we start doing it from birth and carry on until the day we 'die', we assume that it will take care of itself, unless we have a physical problem. We breathe according to what we do with our lives. If we are physical in our work or play, then our lungs will grow. If we are sedentary and smoke a lot then our lungs will be unfit and maybe collapse. Additionally, our lung capacity and function deteriorate with age; therefore all that we can do to improve our breathing will certainly assist us to have a better quality of life.

So why do we need to worry about breathing? If we are training to either become a medium or become a better medium, then we need to oxygenate our brains and body. It will give us more energy and make us more alert. If we are continually tired and lethargic, we cannot do the best communication with the spirit world. We need to be fit! Breathing is something that the majority of us can improve, but as each of us is different, one way may be better than another and the choice must be made accordingly. Therefore, choose your way of learning how to breathe properly and enjoy the experience. This is not a quick fix. It is necessary to maintain correct breathing to be the best we can throughout our lives.

If we do not inhale and exhale efficiently, we will retain a large amount of carbon dioxide in the lungs. This is the gas that should be expelled when breathing out. If we leave a proportion of it in our lungs, then we cannot inhale a full breath. As we get older our breathing and lung capacity naturally deteriorates and with that deterioration, comes a deterioration of health, including life expectancy! We owe it to ourselves to breath properly to live better and longer. The breathing carries oxygen to the brain, so this must also help with our mental abilities. Most people I know say that they would be quite happy to live long, provided that their physical and mental abilities are not deteriorating. Looks like breathing properly could be answer!

An exercise that we incorporate in our circles is rhythmic breathing. It focuses the mind on the actual breathing apparatus. We usually start by asking the students to breathe in to the count of three, hold it for two, breathe out to the count of three and hold it again for two. The mind is then concentrating on what is happening. The awareness is on filling the lungs with good clean air and then exhaling and getting rid of all the nastiness in the lungs. As time goes by, the count changes in a gentle progressive form. The count usually goes up to seven on the inhalation and exhalation, and five on the breath holding. We only limit this because of time and our requirements for our circles.

If the student wishes to take this further, then a good way is to lie on the bed at home and be aware of the breathing. A support for the knees will help any undue stretching of the stomach. The chest area needs thought of both the inbreath and outbreath. It must be noted that any strain is not acceptable. Everything should be gentle. If there are health problems or any other concerns, then a doctor must be consulted. A lot of our energy comes from our breathing, but when you consider that we normally do not breathe properly, we now can be aware of where our energy went.

In a technical sense, the aperture through which we breathe is of a certain size, whether we consider the nose or mouth. We breathe through our mouths when we want more air (oxygen). If we use the rhythmic breathing we can inhale so much more efficiently than normally. Air takes a finite time to go through our mouth or nose. If we want more in our lungs, then the time element must change. Quick breaths will not help, as we have not got rid of the carbon dioxide in our lungs. Breathing deeply and slowly will ensure that large amounts of oxygen are taken into the lungs and that some waste products are removed by exhaling.

To give clarification, the inbreath brings the oxygen into our bodies, obviously this is essential. The outbreath gets rid of the carbon dioxide, but when we breathe normally we do not get rid all of it; therefore there are times when we need to be fully conscious of what we are doing. From time to time a good thing to do is to try and get rid of as much of the carbon dioxide by trying to puff it out more than we do normally.

There are many causes for bad breathing and it not always just because we are ill. Emotional and psychological problems can cause stress and prevent us from normal breathing, that is why people 'who know' suggest that we should sit down and breathe consciously so that we can get back to a more normal breathing. The simple formula is, that breathing properly = more oxygen = less stress, may be of help to bring about some degree of calmness.

Health experts are now analysing how we breathe for two main reasons, one is because the incidence of asthma is on the increase, and the other is because life is now more stressful than it was a few years ago. With panic attacks, people tend to hyperventilate. Reverting to steady breathing will help alleviate the problem. Many people work in offices, and this brings its own problems such as lack of exercise, poor breathing and stress. Because many of the buildings that we inhabit are either centrally heated or air-conditioned, this also causes our breathing to be poor. Being hunched over a computer or desk, together with the thought that the job has to be done as quickly as possible, will inhibit breathing. It really does pay dividends to take a couple of minutes out of each hour and breathe properly.

There are many Internet sites where people who know what they are talking about provide information. There are also sites where there are free tests. It seems a very good idea to utilise the sites in order to improve your breathing ability. Some references are given in Chapter 19 for further reading and help.

Sometimes we think about those 'nuts' that go for long walks. They are exercising their lungs better than we are. Not only that, they are fitter than we are. It doesn't take a genius to work out what we need to do as individuals. As with any form of exercise, whether it is breathing exercises or long walks or any other form of exercise that we are not used to—check with your doctor!

Some words of caution. Do not 'push' yourself with breathing or exercise. Be sensible. If you think it right—see your doctor. If you have any breathing difficulties, sit down and recover. If you still have a problem—see your doctor.

CHAPTER 7

HOW TO CREATE ENERGY

SECTION 1 INTRODUCTION

We all know how to expend energy, but many mediums get to the point of either giving a reading, or service or demonstration, and then realise that the energy has run out. It may be that the venue is a new one, and there was anxiety in trying to find where to go, any tenseness prior to the meeting will use up energy. This makes the communication very difficult. Little has been written about creating energy, or even holding on to it when there is some available. Hopefully the information contained here will help to some degree.

The body is the vehicle that we use in our day-to-day life for many things, but it does depend on the energy that it contains. We know the cause of tiredness, in general terms, and that is a lack of energy. Many human beings expend energy without any thought of leaving some for later. This is apparent with the 'binge drinkers' and others who do things to their body that causes the body (and mind) to become distressed. Athletes know very well all that they should do to achieve their goals, but the majority of the rest of us humans do not. In this case, mediums that are entering a challenging field of expertise, need to take the same care of their body and mind in a similar way as an athlete, although maybe not to the same degree.

Talking can be wonderful for boosting your energy level, but there are times when we are talking with someone, maybe who is distressed or just a miserable person, that our level of energy will become depleted. Often, when mediums are giving private readings, and the person who is getting the reading keeps asking questions or cannot understand what is being said, they 'pull' the energy from the medium. Most mediums think of the person who is getting the reading and not themselves, so they let their energy level fall. A stable medium will not allow this to happen, as with the fall of energy, tiredness will take over which can cause other problems. These problems can be the next reading being near useless, or mistakes being made elsewhere.

Sleep is an important start. To benefit from sleep we should look at it as a rational series of steps. We need to go to bed at a reasonable time (this, to a certain extent, has to be balanced against our individual sleep patterns). We need sufficient sleep, which does not mean lazing the day away in bed. Therefore it seems reasonable to go to bed at the same time each night and get up at the same time each morning, after having 6, 7 or 8 hours sleep, depending on our metabolism and age.

Food is the fuel that we use to create energy, so this also requires thought. Breakfast is important to kick start our insides. Until we feed our stomachs, they think that we are still asleep, so we wake it up with food—but not any old food, nor do we need vast quantities at each 'sitting'. A number of small meals are better than one or two huge meals each day. There are many books on healthy eating, and it is not the purpose of this book to cover areas where I have no expertise.

Each of us is made up mainly of water; therefore it is prudent to keep ourselves topped up. We lose a lot of fluid through natural processes, and it is very important not to lose energy, by being dehydrated. Although water is used in making coffee, it is a diuretic and partly negates the water element's beneficial properties. It is far better to drink water on its own. We are all different shapes and sizes, and we may need differing amounts of water, but it seems to be generally accepted that we should consume about one and a half to two litres each day. I am told that during World War Two, the army was rationed to half a pint of water a day in the desert, and they survived on that. I have a theory that we are now asked to drink more water because there are so many additives in our food, and that the water helps to flush out some of those impurities. Maybe this is true, I don't know.

A recent UK published study on tea drinking, says that tea not only rehydrates as well as water does, but it can also protect against heart disease and some cancers, as it contains antioxidants. The study also goes on to say that three to four cups each day are recommended. Maybe the British way of drinking tea has always been a good idea.

Activity is the next aspect, and it is a little difficult to get it exactly right. We need some energy usage in our daily lives, but not to excess. From all sorts of areas comes information about doing cardiovascular exercise, and how often. At the other end of the spectrum is to not do too much at one time. We can use the analogy of a machine when describing the body. We need to keep it running the best way we can, and to do that we cannot force it to do more than it can without a breakdown. We also need to keep it topped up with fuel. Most machines are not run continuously, and so have rest periods. The more that you care for your machine/body the better it will perform.

Using a different analogy with respect to our minds, a computer seems obvious. We need to get the right programme to ensure that we get the right results. We have touched on the hardware (the body), now we have to consider what we are feeding in to the mind. Where there is substandard teaching, the input will not provide a good output. Rubbish in/rubbish out is a well-known metaphor.

SECTION 2 DIFFERENT ASPECTS

BACK TO TALKING ABOUT ENERGY!

There are a number of elements that can provide energy, including sounds of various types, movement, touch, smell and taste. All provided from our own senses. The problem is that we do not normally understand the relevance of what we have. We look at things in their simplistic state, not from a universal use. Taking each of the senses in turn, let's explore what we can do.

SOUND

I had occasion to be with David Thomson in Denmark, and he asked me to provide some energy. My job was to introduce him to an audience made up of Danish nationals, so I started to speak, and as I did so I was aware that spirit had heard the request, and was providing the answer without me being aware of what they were doing. What happened was that I spoke more loudly and faster. This produced the energy that was required and the evening was a success. Other mediums can also use this phenomenon.

At our centre, I often initiate clapping, especially when greeting a medium on platform. This also provides energy, sometimes without anyone else knowing what is going on. I am sure that some readers will think of other forms of noise that can create energy, but sound can also dissipate energy, especially if it comes as an unexpected noise, making the people hearing it 'jump out of their skins'. At another centre and before the medium demonstrates, a meditation is introduced for about 20 minutes. The problem with that is the congregation becomes lethargic, and the medium has an uphill struggle to provide sufficient energy to make a spiritual contact.

The responses from the congregation/audience also come under this heading. There are people who are not giving any input who want a message. They will drain energy very quickly. It is important not to continue with a message if the response is negative, because the mediums energy will be drained. Although there is an inherent need to give good, accurate information it must be balanced with the energy level. Many mediums will move away from a person if they get three 'No's' in succession. A novice medium feels that they must make the point and ensure that the message gets across, but the next message can be in jeopardy if the energy drops too low.

MOVEMENT

As an observer, I have noticed that many mediums unconsciously rub their hands together. This is a way of generating energy. Another way is to pace up and down, with variations of speed, depending on energy requirements. Some mediums go for a brisk walk immediately before their demonstration so that they start their work fully energised.

TOUCH

Some mediums, often without realising why, touch or lean against another person who has energy, and take some for themselves, thereby making their mediumship better. When giving a private reading some mediums touch either the hands or the aura around the hands of the sitter before the reading. Healing (a transfer of energy) is by touch of either the aura or body. I have known a medium who usually does this, and on one occasion, without any knowledge, the sitter (who had eczema, but it was unseen) had a spontaneous clear-up of the symptom. Care needs to be taken though as energy could be taken from the medium, unless they are prepared for it.

The sun also 'touches' us, and many mediums are aware how much easier it is to work when the sun has shined upon them. If the weather is good, such as in Spain or the Canary Islands and many other warm climates, the mediumship works so much better. Weather can make different changes to different mediums, as some can work better in a thunderstorm and some cannot.

SMELL

Smelling salts can jerk our senses into operation, although I do not recommend their use, but extra strong mints can also do the same trick, but not immediately before demonstrating. The clarity of smell is the important part here. Lack of smell will dull mediumship, so any sensible way to ensure that the nose is functioning correctly is as good as gaining energy—it helps gain confidence, especially when perfume or other significant aromas are sensed. Having a cold or a sinus complaint can seriously impair mediumship.

Another de-sensitiser is smoking. It seems strange that in the 'old days' mediums would be smoking while giving a reading, and be very evidential. Nowadays, because the quality of mediumship is generally not so good, any help to have a clear channel must not be ignored. Smoking affects both smell and taste—not only that, the people who are near the medium may also be put off with the smell of stale tobacco. To be the best medium possible, these aspects will, over time, curtail even those with the most determined attitude.

TASTE

A negative aspect is given above, under Smell. That is smoking. It tends to mask our normal taste buds. Another aspect is overeating. With a too full stomach, the blood in the body is used to help the digestive system, taking a large proportion of oxygen away from the brain. The brain/mind needs blood, which carries the oxygen to keep the mediumistic abilities active. With Gordon Higginson, he ate as he wanted, sometimes having a full meal immediately before doing his spiritual work. He was an outstanding exception.

A 'new taste on the block' is catapult coffee. It is advertised as able to energise your physical and mental abilities. I have not tried it yet, but it contains green coffee infused with herbs, with added Yerba Mate, Angelica Sinensis and Guarana powder. This is not advertising this product, but as an indication of what may be available. Some mediums that I know drink Red Bull before demonstrating, others Coke or Pepsi. Maybe a cup of coffee would do the same. As we are all different, maybe each of us needs to find out what does it for us?

Because of general deterioration of health, some mediums that I know take vitamins. I do not advocate taking any supplements of any sort without serious research by each individual. Just because somebody does something to promote their own vitality, does not mean that everybody else should do the same. Common sense should always prevail. If you think that you need a 'pick-me-up', then it would be sensible to contact a professional who knows their job well. Taking supplements without serious thinking could do more harm than good.

The Mind

There is a way of preparing so that a 'quick fix' can be used in an emergency. It consists of taking time to condition the mind. Sit in a chair and become placid in the mind. Imagine sending an extension from your feet through the earth below you (if you are several floors up, just compensate for the distance in your mind). Having reached a definite visualisation, then imagine that at each side of your ankles (to the left of the left one and to the right of the right one) there are two handles. Pull the handles up as far as you can, and at the same time, become aware that you are pulling energy up from the ground into your body.

This needs to be practised fairly often in the initial stages, but eventually, it will become very easy. The 'quick fix' is when you need energy, sit down, imagine the two handles and pull up the energy. It does need the initial conditioning though.

There are other areas that have an impact on our energy. These are:

Emotions

High emotions of whatever kind can drain the energy from our system. Sometimes, when we are on a 'high' it can work to our advantage, but that also digresses from an open mind, which is accepting spirit communication. If we are placid, then spirit impressions can be better sensed. Overall, it is better not to be consumed by emotion if we wish to work in our best way. It is quite normal for a medium that is overshadowed by their guide to occasionally become emotional, but this should not be so all the time.

Fitness

This is an area where we can all take advantage of what is on offer. It is a well-known fact that—strange as it may seem—exercise actually promotes energy. Most people do not wish to take very energetic exercise, but there are many other ways that are also suitable for the physically impaired, and the older generation with their aches and pains. These are Yoga, Tai Chi, Chi Kung and various other slow exercises. These have been mentioned in Chapter 5 Breathing. As you will appreciate, there is a strong connection between exercise and breathing, and both of these need to be done correctly to enable us, as human machines, to operate at our peak performance. I came across another way of improving ourselves the other day, promoting Yog and Pranayam. Practitioners claim benefits to the physical, mental and spiritual aspects of themselves. I have given the reference in Chapter 19.

ACUPUNCTURE

The Chinese believe that in our bodies, energy (or Chi) flows. Sometimes these flows are interrupted and by stimulating one or more of the 700 acupuncture points, the flow can be restored. There are many books and practitioners to follow up this line of research.

LIGHT

Sunlight is a great help towards a healthy and energetic body. Obviously, there is a great need for caution, especially where skin cancer and sunburn are possibilities. In older times, sun bathing (I have separated the two words deliberately) was helpful to people who were recovering from illness, and those wanting to enhance their general health. It is no wonder that a tanned person looks healthy, provided all protective precautions have been observed. Recently, studies have shown that people who shun sunlight altogether are low in Vitamin D. We do need *some* sunlight on our bodies.

Some people suffer from lethargy and depression during the winter months. This is known as Seasonal Affective Disorder (SAD) and can be combated by using a special light source. This is about 10 times the intensity of ordinary domestic lighting. To put it in perspective, domestic lighting can be around 200 to 500 lux, and a bright summer's day around 100,000 lux. SAD boxes provide about 2,500 lux. This can replace some of the energy to the body if used for one to four hours a day. Obviously, the maker's instructions must be followed.

Auras

Although we all have auras, we cannot change them except through the change that we can make within our physical selves because the aura is like a reflection of how we feel. Auras (also known as 'breath of air') react to events around us. If we enter into a heated debate, our aura will change. If we are given healing our aura will change. We react to light, sound and everything that vibrates around us. If we have a TV in our bedroom and other electrical items, then again we will react to it—usually by not sleeping very well.

Biorythms

This is based on the premise that every person's life moves in cycles. It views three energy levels: physical, emotional and intellectual. Each of these has a different cycle. The physical has a 23-day cycle, the emotional a 28-day cycle and the intellectual a 33-day cycle. The start date is the day that we were born.

Using the information available, we can each work out when our good and bad days are. In that way we can have a better understanding of ourselves and how we interact with each other, and more importantly when we have good energy, and when we need to do something about a lack of it.

Living

The most important thing that we can do about our energies is to go for a walk. It is the simplest of exercises, anyone can do it (with certain exceptions) and the benefits are very worth-while. If we maintain our body, mind and emotions in a reasonable state, then we are doing ourselves one of the greatest favours possible. Not only that, the quality of our mediumship and communication with spirit, in whatever form, will be much improved.

To sum up, there are many causes for lack of energy, but there are also many ways in which we can improve. It is my earnest thought that anyone who works for spirit, in whatever way, should never run short of energy. I have seen it happen many times causing much disappointment for many people. There is an answer, so please use what is best for you.

CHAPTER 8

MEDITATION

INTRODUCTION

I believe that meditations are to achieve a set purpose. I do not believe that just sitting with an empty mind achieves anything, as thoughts will turn to everyday problems and the time is lost. Because of this, I have given each meditation the purpose at the beginning, so that they may be chosen with a better understanding. All meditations should be given sufficient pauses to ensure that the students follow the words and also have time to achieve all of the objectives that are given. Each meditation should have safety procedures built in. For instance, if the meditation incorporates getting into a boat, assurances must be made about safety, because some people are afraid of water and maybe they cannot swim. This causes a level of stress that inhibits relaxation. I have used all these meditations over the years with great success.

Each meditation should be started in the same way, therefore I recommend using the Egyptian meditation position. This is with a fairly straight back, head erect, feet flat on the floor and the hands loosely resting in the lap.

Ideally, a recording should be made, using the words that are here as a basis. It would be far better to use somebody's voice that is acceptable to you or those who are listening. There is a need to allow pauses as the meditation progresses. I am quite happy that anyone who wants to use these meditations for the purpose of spiritual enhancement may use them. The principle with which I work, is to help people.

When a medium is experienced, there may be an understanding that meditation is no longer necessary. Because with many mediums they have done the exercises before, there may be no need to sit and meditate before any work is done. There are a few mediums who never meditate, but they are in the minority.

MEDITATIONS

MEETING A FRIEND IN THE SPIRIT WORLD.

Adopt the Egyptian meditation position. This is with a fairly straight back, head erect, feet flat on the floor and the hands loosely resting in the lap. Imagine that you are in a log cabin, which has a chair that you are sitting on, a window to your left and a door in front of you. There is a knock at the door. You ask the person outside to enter. The door opens and a friend from the spirit world enters and greets you. They now ask you to go with them outside the cabin.

As you leave the cabin, be aware of the sights, sounds and smells that can impinge on your senses. There are trees and bushes, together with flowers, birds and small animals. There is nothing to harm you. You follow your friend along a pathway, which descends slightly. In the distance there is a waterfall, and as you approach it the sound increases. As you round a corner, there in front of you is the waterfall with two rocks near it, one being slightly smaller than the other. As your gaze moves around, you will see that the waterfall empties into a beautiful lake, which is crystal clear. At the far side are various animals drinking.

Your friend sits on the larger of the two rocks and indicates to you that you may sit on the smaller rock. Spend a little time getting to know your friend and do not be shy of asking questions. You may wish to enquire about your friend's background and also ask how the two of you will work together. When it is time, I will come back to you, but enjoy this time together.

About 7 to 15 minutes should elapse before continuing, depending on the stage of development.

There will be a slight change now. Your friend suggests that you take a swim in the lake. There is nothing to fear; in fact you can swim under water and still breathe quite normally. Do not worry about your clothes, you will find that they are waterproof. Enjoy the time in the water and be aware that you are being refreshed. Look around and see the fish swimming with you. When you come out of the water, you will find that your clothes are instantly dry.

Go back to the rocks and you and your friend will then make your way back along the path that you previously came down. Be aware of all the sights sounds and smells as you both return. At the door to the cabin, your friend will say goodbye and then go off into a different direction. You now enter the cabin, close the door and sit back down on the seat you were previously sitting on. You may now come back to the reality of this room and open your eyes.

Time is required to enquire as to what happened with each sitter, if in a group.

This is the finish of this meditation

MEETING ANGELS

This is a short meditation from the speaking point of view, and longer for the time left alone. Its impact is surprising.

Adopt the Egyptian meditation position. Be aware that there is a knock on the door. You open it to find an angel standing just outside. The angel's hand is outstretched for you to take. This is a rare chance to go with an angel and to see whatever it is that is to be shown to you. Take the hand. The angel will take you up into the air. I do not know where you are going, but I do know that you will be perfectly safe.

About 10 to 15 minutes should elapse before continuing, depending on the stage of development.

Be aware that you need to return to where you and the angel started. Allow the angel to bring you back to the door from where you left. Thank the angel for taking you, close the door and sit in the seat that you were sitting before. You may now come back to the reality of this room and open your eyes.

Time is required to enquire as to what happened with each sitter, if in a group.

This is the finish of this meditation

MEETING A LOVED ONE

Adopt the Egyptian meditation position. As you sit there, imagine that you are sitting on a tree stump. In front of you is the sea, with a small wooden jetty close by. Behind and around you is what you would expect to see. Walk towards the jetty and you will see that there is a small boat tied to it. Walk out onto the jetty and get into the boat. Notice that there are plenty of cushions in the boat. Untie the rope that is securing the boat to the jetty and lay down, using the cushions to make yourself comfortable. You will not feel seasick or upset by the movement of the sea.

Look up and see a few small clouds in the sky. The sun is shining and there is a breeze. Use your mind to adjust the sun and breeze so that the temperature is comfortable. The boat drifts. If you wish, you can put your hand over the side and feel the texture of the water and its temperature. If you look carefully you may see a seagull or some other bird. Everything is peaceful.

After a while, there is a little bump and you realise that the boat has touched sand. Get up and look around. Behind the beach are trees and bushes, some with beautiful blooms. Away off to the right is a pathway. You are aware of the boat again and realise that you have to pull it up the beach. You get out of the boat and find that you need very little exertion to move it. As you get out of the boat be aware of the water that is up to your ankles. Now that the boat is safe, you experience the sand between your toes.

Because it seems the obvious thing to do, you walk along the beach towards the pathway. There may be exotic birds flying around the trees. You look towards the pathway and realise that someone is coming towards you, but at the moment cannot distinguish who. As you get closer, you realise that it is somebody that you have missed for a long time. Someone that you love. You run towards each other and embrace. You both then go to the pathway and leave the beach behind. I will leave you for a while so that you may have time together. I will come back for you in a little while.

About 7 to 15 minutes should elapse before continuing, depending on the stage of development.

Be aware that it is time to return to the beach. Both of you make your way back along the pathway and towards the boat. When you reach the boat, both of you push the boat into the water. You now say your goodbyes and you get into the boat. The person who has been with you gives the boat a push, turns and walks back the way that you have come. You watch until they are nearly at the pathway, they turn and wave. You respond. Then there is nobody on the beach, so you settle yourself down in the boat on the cushions and relax. The time goes fairly quickly as you think of all that has happened. You are aware of the sun and breeze, the odd cloud in the sky and if you wish to put your hand in the water as you drift, you may. You then become aware that you are back at the jetty, so you tie the boat securely to it and get out of the boat. Walk back to the tree stump on which you were sitting previously. Be aware of your surroundings. Now you may now come back to the reality of this room and open your eyes.

Time is required to enquire as to what happened with each sitter, if in a group.

This is the finish of this meditation

GETTING AN IMPORTANT MESSAGE FROM SPIRIT

Adopt the Egyptian meditation position. Imagine that you are sitting on a low bough of a tree, which is quite safe. The tree is in a field and has some blooms on it. There are lots of flowers in the field of different colours. In the middle distance is a hedgerow with birds flying in and out of them. Behind you is a pathway that goes up an incline between some bushes. You get up and walk up the pathway and as you do so, you are aware of small animals in the bushes, and the heady scent of blossoms.

As you go up the pathway, it gets steeper, but you do not find it difficult. Other people from different pathways join yours. When you reach the top, you can see a large valley. There are many pathways from all directions, each centring on one large field. Hundreds of people are making their way down there, wearing many bright colours, and sit on the ground facing towards one corner. More people join your pathway. They are speaking in many different languages, but all are going to the field.

When you get to the field, find yourself a convenient position and sit down facing the same corner as everyone else. When all the people are assembled, there is a sudden quiet. All are intently looking towards the corner of the field. A bright white light seems to hover there. From the white light each person can see someone who they revere. A voice speaks to each person at the same time, although those sitting in the field hear only one voice, just the same as you.

What you hear is for your own self and nobody else. It is an important communication from spirit.

About 3 to 5 minutes should elapse before continuing, depending on the stage of development.

When the communication has finished, there still seems to be quietness in the field, and then all the languages of the world start speaking. Everyone then gets up and makes their way back the way they came. You look around and see lines of people making their way back to where they came from. As you make your way back, be aware of all that is happening. Walk back up the hill to the top, have a last look at the other people going in different directions.

Walk over the crest of the hill and down the other side, passing everything that you passed on the way up. Return to the field from where you started and make your way over to the bough and sit back on it. Be aware of your surroundings. You may now come back to the reality of this room and open your eyes.

> *Time is required if the sitter wishes to talk about their experiences, if in a group.*

This is the finish of this meditation

LOOKING AT YOUR LIFE—PAST AND FUTURE

Adopt the Egyptian meditation position. Imagine that you are sitting in a field under a large chestnut tree. Although the sun is warm, there is a cooling breeze, which you can alter to suit you. The grass is about half a metre high and as you look around, there are many flowers of different colours; also there are other trees a little way off and some bushes with beautiful flowers.

You get up and on the other side of the tree there is a pathway going up a hill, so you walk towards it. As you do so, be aware of the sounds of birds and the beautiful colours around you. The pathway becomes steeper, but you find that there is no difficulty in walking. When you get to the top of the hill there is a clearing and beyond that a sheer cliff going straight up. In the face of the cliff is a large door, and as you approach it you can see some words over the top of the door. When you are close enough you can see what it says. ***Knowledge is power***.

Go up to the door and use the large knocker to let whoever is inside that you wish to enter. The door opens and you meet a person dressed in a long white robe with a cowl over their head. They open the door wide and ask you to enter. Once inside, the doorkeeper closes the door. Inside there is a large table with chairs at each side, and beyond that it seems to be a very large library.

Your attention is now focused on the doorkeeper, and now you realise that it is **your** doorkeeper. Your doorkeeper pushes back their cowl and you can see them clearly. You are asked what period of your life you wish to know about. Think carefully as you only get one choice at this time. Take your time and make your mind up very carefully. Do you wish to know more about something that happened in your past? Do you wish to know what is happening now? Or do you wish to know something of your future?

Having made up your mind, your doorkeeper goes into the library and returns with a large book. On the outside in gold lettering is your full name, together with another inscription of past, present or future. Yours has the appropriate one for which you asked. Before you go further, ensure that you have the right question in your mind, so that you know exactly what you need to know. You may now sit at the table and open the book. I shall leave you for a while and will come back for you a little later.

About 10 to 15 minutes should elapse before continuing, depending on the stage of development.

Be aware that you now need to return. Close your book and give it back to your doorkeeper. Thank them and go towards the door. The door is opened and you leave. When outside the door is closed, and you may feel that you would like to know more or should have asked a different question, but there is always the possibility of returning here at a later time.

Return along the pathway that you took to get to the top of the hill. The return is much easier and you soon find yourself back under the chestnut tree where you began. Be aware of your surroundings. Now you may now come back to the reality of this room and open your eyes.

Time is required if the sitter wishes to talk about their experiences, if in a group.

This is the finish of this meditation

EXPLORING SPIRIT HALLS OF LEARNING

Adopt the Egyptian meditation position. Be aware of the place in which you are sitting. Let your mind focus on the roof of the building that you are in, and as you do, be aware that your thought puts you there on the top of the roof. You are perfectly safe with nothing to fear. You are not dizzy. You are not afraid of heights. I am caring for you.

Now that you have regained your composure, look around and you will see many small clouds. One of them is coming towards you and stops right by your side. A canopy opens and you can see inside the cloud. There is a seat that looks as though it was made just for you. Get inside and make yourself comfortable. There is a seatbelt there especially for you, so put it on and feel quite safe, then the canopy closes. The cloud moves away and at the same time goes higher. The view is magnificent.

While the view keeps your attention, take a moment to see where you are going. The cloud has moved away from earth and is approaching some sort of heavenly structure. You can see very wide golden steps in the foreground. The cloud approaches the steps and stops right beside them. The canopy opens; you take off your seat belt and get out onto the steps. Once you are out, the canopy in the cloud closes and the cloud moves away. It gives the impression that it is like a taxi.

Climb the steps and you will find yourself in a large hall. There are notices that are very clear. They point in different ways for various types of learning. Choose one and let's explore. The one that you have chosen goes along some corridors and then you arrive at the room for the subject that you have chosen. The room is different to our normal concept. There are no walls, but you cannot see into any other room. There are other people in the room, as well as you. One person seems to be teaching, but they are not speaking. You find a seat and make yourself comfortable.

In your mind somebody says 'welcome', and you now realise that your learning is done through the mind. Each person in the room is not hearing the same thing. Each person is being taught at their speed so that they can assimilate information without any additional stress. Spend some time here if you wish, or go to another room. I will leave you for a while to explore, but I will come back for you when it is time to go.

About 10 to 15 minutes should elapse before continuing, depending on the stage of development.

Be aware that it is time to return. A notice will tell you which way to go to get to the steps. Meet me there. As you come down the steps your cloud is waiting for you. The canopy opens and you can see the seat that (again) looks as though it was made just for you. Get inside and make yourself comfortable. The seatbelt is there, so put it on and feel quite safe, then the canopy closes. The cloud moves away. As you look back, the heavenly structure seems to fade away and then you are aware that you are approaching earth. Be aware of the lights and anything else that you may see. The cloud seems to know exactly where it is going, because it arrives at the roof from where you left. The canopy opens you remove your seat belt, and you get out of the cloud. You are perfectly safe with nothing to fear. You are not dizzy. You are not afraid of heights. With the thought that the chair you were sitting in is just below you, you are in the chair. Be aware of your surroundings. Now you may now come back to the reality of this room and open your eyes.

Time is required if the sitter wishes to talk about their experiences, if in a group.

This is the finish of this meditation

Observation of self

Adopt the Egyptian meditation position. Visualise being at the seaside, sitting on the top of cliffs, looking out to sea. The sea is calm; the weather is sunny with a cool breeze. Just a little way from the shore is a curiously shaped structure with a door in it. Without any problems, and perfectly safely, allow yourself, very much like a leaf, to just drift down to the beach at the bottom of the cliffs. Walk along the beach, being aware of the sand crunching between your toes, until you are opposite the structure in the sea. When you are in line with it, notice that just below the surface of the sea there is a pathway leading out to the structure.

Without hesitation, walk along the pathway, being aware of the water lapping up to your ankles. The further out you go, the pathway remains at the same depth, with the water still just up to your ankles. You are quite safe. When you get to the structure, open the door and look inside. Inside, there is a stairway going down. There are handholds on both sides and the stairs are not too steep. The lighting inside is just at the right level for you. Close the door and go down the stairs. There is nothing to fear at all.

You come to a landing and another set of stairs. Keep going down and down, being quite safe. Down you go until you reach a large cavern. Inside and to one side there is a chair on a platform, so go and sit on it. Opposite you there is a stage. The lights dim, but you can still see clearly. In front of you there seems to be a huge television screen, but it allows you to see whatever happens in 3D.

There is a scene in front of you. You may see yourself now or a little later. You are there only as an observer. You cannot become involved as much as you may want to. Watch what happens. You may see yourself in a different way to that which you previously thought. Watch how you react to various things and situations. You may see somebody that you know either in the spirit world or in the material. Do not be concerned, just watch. I will leave you for a little while, and I **will** come back.

About 7 to 10 minutes should elapse before continuing, depending on the stage of development.

The scene in front of you fades away. The lighting returns to its previous level. You realise that it is time to return, so you get out of the chair and go to the bottom of the stairs. The ascent is not as hard as you might think. Remember there are handrails at each side of the stairs. Although the stairs go up and up, you can easily walk up them. You reach the landing and then go up the next flight of stairs. When you reach the top, take a moment before you open the door. Slowly open the door until your eyes are accustomed to the sunlight. Step outside and then close the door.

Walk back along the pathway, which is still at the same depth as before. When you reach the beach, notice that your feet are now touching sand and not water. With just a thought that you want to be at the top of the cliffs, you are there. Go back to where you were sitting at the top of the cliffs.

Be aware of your surroundings. Now you may now come back to the reality of this room and open your eyes.

Time is required if the sitter wishes to talk about their experiences, if in a group.

This is the finish of this meditation

TALKING TO THE ANIMALS

Why? Because animals have been on earth for as long as us, if not more, and we expect them to understand our commands, but never think about listening to them.

Adopt the Egyptian meditation position. Relax and be aware that there is nothing scary going to happen. Nearly everyone has been to a zoo, but if not, it's not hard to visualise. Visualise a place where animals live. Not all are compatible, so there is some segregation. You are visiting the zoo, and go to the animals that you feel comfortable with. Sit down with your choice and allow your mind to reach out. First of all consider their feelings. Are they happy as a group? Now look at just one of the group.

Allow your mind to link with the animal. Sense its mood. Understand if they are happy or sad. Send a thought asking if it will communicate with you. Animals are not stupid, and the one that you have chosen looks at you and you feel a response. Spend time exploring the life of this animal. Its likes and dislikes. Talk with your mind. Be receptive. Enjoy the time together.

> *About 2 to 3 minutes should elapse before continuing, depending on the stage of development.*

Thank the animal for taking the time to communicate with you and move on to another animal that is different. Again make contact and understand what they are and what they are about.

> *About 2 to 3 minutes should elapse before continuing, depending on the stage of development.*

Again, thank the animal for taking time to communicate with you. Now spend a little time to understand what has happened, not only to the animal, but also to you.

> *About 2 to 3 minutes should elapse before continuing, depending on the stage of development.*

Bring the memories back with you. Be aware of your surroundings. Now you may now come back to the reality of this room and open your eyes.

> *Time is required if the sitter wishes to talk about their experiences, if in a group.*

This is the finish of this meditation (and the chapter)

CHAPTER 9

PSYCHIC WORK

What does psychic mean? Psychic is defined as outside the possibilities of natural laws, such as mental telepathy. Or, a person who is sensitive to parapsychological forces or influences. It is not 'being a medium'.

When you are aware that you know the 'phone is going to ring, and you know who it is—that is psychic. It is NOT a communication from the spirit world—well unless you are very lucky! If you feel that a person next to you is feeling ill, that is psychic. Any awareness that you pick up from another person is psychic. If you touch something that belongs to another person (alive or dead), and you get certain feelings, that is psychic. On the other hand, it is possible that if you can hold something belonging to someone who is dead, it can **lead** to a link with a person in the spirit world.

With regard to *leading* to a link, let us consider the Tarot, although it is not even psychic within the meaning of the word. Many things have been said and written about the Tarot, but essentially it is a tool for divination, although if used in conjunction with a spiritual connection and *using psychic abilities* tuned into the sitter, quite a lot of positive information can be provided. There are many designs of Tarot cards, all of which are provided with instructions. The problem is then, why should we use someone else's interpretation, for something that you will be doing. We each interpret everything in this world differently than anyone else, so you need to use your own interpretation.

I have taught Tarot over a number of years, and although I get very good results, I maintain that the only way of learning how to use them is to take (say) three cards each evening; look at them very closely and after inspecting every detail, decide what each minute detail means to you. Work through the whole pack in that manner, then consider what spread should be used and try out a dummy reading. When using the cards for a reading, not all the details will be apparent, therefore the reading will only contain details that seem to be outstanding, and also relevant. The same principle holds good for the many other methods of divination. This is divination, not psychic work.

We need to be able to use a certain amount of psychic ability in our life as a working medium, but we need to discriminate carefully. Within a circle, the sitters could provide an item each, which are placed under a cloth on a tray. Each could then pick an item that does not belong to them and then sense what information the item has.

Another exercise is to place a simple picture or a Zener card into envelopes, so that the envelope can be held and the content can be psychometrised. A variation is to put small objects, wrapped in paper, into glass tubes so that they cannot be seen and then psychometrise them.

Psychic information can arrive in a number of ways, such as by touch (either actual or perceived), through our emotions, by hearing (either actual or perceived), through sight (either actual or perceived), through smell or by sensing.

When meeting someone for the first time, we normally shake hands. This touch of hands will give rise to a sensation that can be interpreted as being good or not good, or somewhere in between. With some experience, the sensation can be better attuned, so that more information is derived. It is possible to make the link strong enough so that you will know **why** you either like or dislike someone.

By the touch of hands, you can be aware of the mental state of the other person. They, without showing any symptoms on the outside, can be discerned as happy or sad, depressed or elated. By the same token, others can also 'pick up' on us!

Now that you have a pretty good idea what psychic is, the next step is to explore how we can learn to do it. There are a number of ways that will work and we can also have some fun with. As with everything we can play about and have fun, but later, when the understanding of the mechanics has been absorbed, the serious application can be used. All of these work, but there should be a conscious understanding as to whether this is for fun or for real.

Let us start with sand readings. All that is required is a large shallow tray with some fine sand on it, about 1 or 2 centimetres thick. One person places their hands on the sand for a few seconds, allowing an imprint—not only of their hands, but also their personality. Another person then places their hands over the imprint and tries to sense whatever might be there. All sensations are then spoken out loud and verified (or not) by the original person. With practice this will work very well.

For the fun part, we tend to do this within a group, and can be used in circles if the psychic aspect is being used. One person who is either selected or volunteered, puts on a blindfold, so that nobody else can be seen. Another person then places their hands on the sand. Because there is a likelihood of some noise from that person (brushing the sand off their hands), then the other people in the room all make some sort of noise to mask the 'giveaway sound'. The tray is then placed on the lap of the person doing the reading.

At this point there is a choice of either leaving the blindfold on or removing it. If it is left on there is a minimum of distraction, and a better aid to concentration. The person then provides information. If this is done in a group or circle, the leader will then reply. The person who originally placed their hands on the sand uses hand signals to signify yes, no or don't know (thumb up, thumb down, wobble hand), so that the reader does not know who they are reading for. When the information is exhausted, the reader is asked as to who the original person was, before removing the blindfold. It can be surprising as to how much information can be gained, and also to find out whom the original person was.

This procedure, with more seriousness, can be used for ascertaining other information in different situations. It could be used to help find someone, by holding an article that was owned by the missing person (provided that it had not been 'contaminated' with other people's information). There are many applications, but the difference between 'playing' in a group or circle, and a serious use is through much practice and serious application.

Another way of practicing is for each person who sits together to bring an item of jewellery or other small object. This is placed under a covered tray as the individuals arrive, not allowing the others to be aware of any item except their own. When the time comes, each individual is asked to take one item without anyone else seeing, and not to take their own item.

Depending on how the leader operates, a certain amount time is required for 'tuning in', and this can be altogether, singly or by splitting everyone up into pairs, so that they work together. Each person requires a finite amount of time and this can alter depending on how much experience each person has. I would suggest no more than 10 minutes initially, decreasing to about 2 to 3 minutes as they become more proficient. In the initial stages it is prudent to advise the people that it is an experiment, because some may have the feeling that what is said is absolutely true, and it may not be.

Flower readings are quite interesting. This can be used within a circle setting as it does provide the use of some aspects of clairsentience; although it's primary use is for psychic work. Each individual is asked to bring a flower complete with some stem. Another person is doing the reading for the one that brought it. It may be that there are a couple of leaves, which could be interpreted as two children, the length of the stem could relate to time, the flower could relate to an individual and the colour could relate to the personality of that person. I have used the word *could* advisedly, as each person doing the reading may interpret in totally differing ways.

Scrying is another way of using psychic ability. The object used for scrying can be a bowl of water, a mirror or some reflecting surface with a black background. It is very similar to using a crystal ball. The way that it is done is by allowing the focus of the eyes to slip, while looking into the scrying surface. The result, which not everyone can achieve, is more subjective rather than objective. From this scrying, there are many possible outcomes, including 'visions' of the future, the past or the present. Here again, the mind is a very powerful tool. By using the mind as a reference, the situation can be set up so that time can be controlled.

Some mediums, when doing a reading, often either touch or nearly touch the hands of the sitter before commencing the reading. This is to obtain a psychic connection. It is quite possible to tune into someone and obtain all sorts of information. The problem with this is you may be encroaching upon personal details that really ought not be divulged. With training, much information can be gleaned from another person without them being aware, although we, as humans, have the basics as part of our makeup. This is why, in a demonstration of mediumship, if a medium relies solely on psychic work, they can do it much more easily than connecting with spirit.

As part of an exercise to enable the sensing of spirit, I use the chair in the corner routine. This is where a chair is placed facing into a corner, and the person being tested is blindfolded and sitting in the chair. I stand behind with my hands on their shoulders, asking if they can feel me standing behind them. The obviously say that they can, so I then remove my hands and pose the same question. Usually the answer is that they can. I then step back one pace and again ask the same question. From this point the answers can change depending on the sensitivity of the person sitting in the chair.

With as little noise as possible I then substitute another person, allowing my own sounds of movement to cover any other sounds. I then ask if there is anyone standing behind—they know that it is not me as I have my voice coming from a different direction. If the answer is that they can, I then ask if it is male or female. From this point I vary how many people are standing behind the chair (up to four) and which gender they are. If they give good answers, I then 'push' a little harder by asking the person in the chair to identify the person or persons standing behind, and also asking for the order that they are in. The main thing to remember is that movement can sometimes be detected easily, and therefore 'masking' sounds need to be employed.

The above exercise is purely psychic, but the application is for the individuals to sense spiritual beings when they come close.

CHAPTER 10

SPIRITUAL WORK

What I mean by spiritual work is only that which deals with spirit (not psychic) and in this chapter, not dealing with physical (trance and materialisation) work. So the included topics are: Clairvoyance, Clairaudience and Clairsentience. Often this is called Mental Mediumship. I will repeat some of that which is contained in Chapter 5, Circles, so that you do not have to keep looking back in the book.

Clairvoyance is the awareness that is obtained via the brow chakra, or third eye. It is possible for some mediums (not all) to see visions provided by the spirit world. Sometimes these visions are nebulous and hard to decipher and sometimes one may be able to see a spirit person just as one would a person in this earthly world. Traditionally, one would expect to see a person in the spirit world and describe them to the recipient of a spiritual message. This would then provide 'evidence' that there is life after death.

Clairaudience is the ability to hear someone in the spirit world, but the way that this is apparent is not always the same. Sometimes it is as though someone was speaking 'in your head' and sometimes it is very similar to our natural hearing. When clairaudience is combined with clairvoyance, a much more positive appreciation may be given of the person who is trying to communicate.

What I would expect from a medium would be a description of the person who wants to communicate through the medium to me, followed by information that they (spirit) wish to impart. This would be clairvoyance followed by clairaudience.

Clairsentience is the ability to 'feel' the spirit person, including what they may have to say. It sounds impossible, but I can assure you that it is so. Many mediums mostly work with clairsentience, with bits of the other two abilities. To be honest, if all three abilities are available, then the work of being a medium is much easier.

To commence with people who have no idea about spiritual communication, it is best approached via the question; have you ever felt an intense dislike or very strong attraction for someone? This is clairsentience. A feeling. If pushed, there may be extra information available which is unseen by the naked eye, but is certainly sensed.

The biggest problem that I have, is the morality of the medium. In an ideal world everyone would be 'nice', but as we are acutely aware, this world is not like that. Therefore, the student should be aware that they ought to apply a moral aspect to their learning. There was a lady a few years ago, that lived in Somerset, who had classified herself as a medium and was quite famous. A number of times she had told female sitters that their husbands would be dead within a few weeks. Needless to say, these ladies were distraught, and sought out my wife for either confirmation or denial. In each case it was totally untrue. Two of the ladies, who my wife did not see, eventually ended up in a mental institution. Each medium is responsible for what they utter, whether it is actually their own words or spirit inspired. If we are to have any standing in our community, we must adhere to reasonable actions. If we denigrate what we do, we not only do that for ourselves, but all who follow us.

To put it into perspective, I work for the highest source, and would never consciously denigrate either what I do or the people in spirit who I do it for. I am not perfect, but I continually strive to be better all the time. I urge all who read this book to do the same.

There are those in the spirit world who are attracted to us as individuals, who wish to help in our development. These are called by various names; spirit guide, doorkeeper, etcetera. I prefer to just call them 'friends', for that is the only word that, for me, fits. They are far closer than our closest friends in this earthly world. Having worked with them, and after some time passes, there is a fantastic rapport that can be used in many ways, provided that it is not abused.

Depending on the closeness of our friend(s), they can sometimes help us with problems, with spiritual information and with guidance for others. The development of that closeness takes time. Think how long it takes to develop a friendship on this earth to a situation of total trust. It all takes time and that time is very precious. If we use it well then we will become a better person. Some of our friends will change. If we relate our development to a schoolroom, as we progress, we change teachers, and so it is with our spiritual friends. Some we retain, and with others, they and we, move on.

To work with a friend in the spirit world, there has to be some communication both ways. The biggest problem is how to know who your friend is, how they communicate with you, and who they are. There are a number of ways of doing this, but this method has been tried and tested for a long time. The parameters of this exercise are set in a closed circle. Appropriate music should be played.

CONTACTING A FRIEND IN THE SPIRIT WORLD WHO WILL WORK WITH YOU.

Sit in the Egyptian meditation position, with the eyes closed. If necessary, go through a relaxation procedure to ensure complete composure. When this has been achieved, the circle leader will then give the following instructions. There needs to be sufficient pauses for the student to allow their minds to absorb not only the information from the circle leader, but also that which is being provided by spirit.

> Prepare your mind to want to contact a friend in the spirit world. There is no need for fear or apprehension. This is a

perfectly normal phenomenon. Be aware of a change of feeling situated around your right shoulder. Stretch your mind to be aware that the feeling is comfortable and that you are aware of someone who is friendly at your right shoulder. Ask your new friend to provide one of the following: a name (this is usually not given at this stage), an aroma of some sort, a touch on the face, hair or on the shoulder. This is for future identification purposes, as there is a more comfortable feeling when there is a built-up rapport.

Ask the students to retain the feeling of someone at their shoulder, and then ask them to open their eyes, while you discuss what has taken place. Take each student through all of their experiences, so that by speaking out loud of what has ensued, they will build a stronger memory of the contact.

Take the students back to the eyes closed situation, and then give them time to communicate with their new-found friend. Suggest that basic questions may be asked where the answers are simple, such as a 'yes' or 'no'. These questions could be about how tall or short, how fat or thin the new friend is, or even in what area will this new friend work with the student. They need to be kept simple, without any undue pressure. At the end of the session, ask the students to thank their new friend for making the contact with them and ask them to leave. Remind the students that this exercise can be repeated numerous times for the purpose of getting to know the new friend.

At a later date, this exercise can be used again, and by changing the parameters slightly, different friends can be introduced, who will work in different spiritual areas.

Because we are all different, each of us cannot always do the same as everyone else, so there needs to some flexibility in the approach of contacting our spirit friends. Some people can visualise easily, while others may take some time to reach that ability. A variation on meeting spirit friends is to ask the students to visualise a bridge that they find themselves comfortable with (some students do not like high bridges and some do not like a lot of water running underneath, and other variations).

Ask them to imagine that the centre is higher than the two ends and that the colour of the bridge is just like a rainbow. Set the scene around the bridge to be full of flowers and shrubs. Invite the students to slowly walk to the centre of the bridge, being aware of all the beautiful colours. Ask them to stop at the centre and await their spirit guide or friend to meet them at the centre. Once they have met, from there they can go to either side of the bridge and what happens next will be left to their imagination. Although imagination is not quite the right word, I hesitate to use any other, as often the response seems quite real. Sometimes it is real and sometimes not. We all want to impress our peers, but sometimes our imagination gets in the way! Remember to bring the students back to the centre of the bridge, say their goodbyes and then return to where they started.

An area of spiritual work that is gaining interest is under the misnomer of *Psychic Art*. Strictly speaking, it is not psychic as it is spirit inspired. There are a number of different approaches to learning about this subject, but here I will give a simplistic approach. First of all the preparation must be done, which includes having paper, pencil, eraser, pencil sharpener and a board to rest the paper on. The paper texture choice will change over time, but in the initial stages, plain A4 paper is fine. The next piece of preparation is to sit somewhere comfortable, with support for your board, and then allow yourself to become relaxed.

Send a thought to the spirit world that you wish to become an artist for spirit and would someone come and help you. My way of moving from this position is to look at the paper and allow the eyes to see something on the paper. If this is really difficult, then change to a very rough texture paper. It is a similar situation as looking into a fire and seeing pictures, although nowadays fires have given way to looking at walls and clouds. See a picture—the mind needs a certain amount of control, as the pictures that can be seen should be limited to animals or people. Some aspect of the outline should be visible, so trace the outline that you see. You may start from the centre or the outside. It does not matter. Allow your mind to pick up all aspects available and complete the picture.

The way that the pencil is held may be different from normal. Try different techniques of holding the pencil, you will eventually come up the way that is right both for you and your inspirer. Remember that as in any other learning process, the teacher may change. Some people will progress slowly and achieve an acceptable level of art, while others may find that their hand/arm movement is out of their control, but in spirit's control. Regardless of progression, try other drawing mediums, such as pastels, crayons or ink. Try the different textures of paper. It is all a learning process, which can both be fun and immensely helpful to others. What a wonderful gift to be able to draw another person's loved one or pet.

While drawing, there may be other pieces of random information popping into your head. Write these down at the side of the paper. They may well contain supporting evidence that makes the picture mean so much more. Working with spirit is very rewarding, especially when you make a contact for someone on the earth plane with their loved one in the spirit world.

Occasionally there are other ways that spirit can communicate. One of these is by impressing someone who is interested in music to write music pieces. Well-known composers, at times, impress those who can work with them. In this instance I feel that this is not a subject that we can control, but if you are on the same wavelength as a spirit person, they may come to you to express their talent. It is their choice though.

CHAPTER 11

PLATFORM WORK AND DEMONSTRATIONS

These are the phrases that are used when mediums either work in a church or centre carrying out a service (platform work), or a demonstration of mediumship. Both aspects are in front of an audience, where mediumship is attempted. Factually, mediums are not perfect. They try and give evidence of spiritual survival so that the recipient may have some feeling that their loved one is still interested in their welfare. Sometimes there is a breakdown of communication (just like a telephone) and either the message does not get through, or there is some distortion by the mediums mind. It must be said that the quality of evidence amongst the 'good' mediums is extraordinary.

Most churches recognise that not everyone can present a reading, an address AND demonstrate mediumship, so there are some mediums that work together when taking a service. Some churches only accept one medium, which is a pity as it may preclude two excellent mediums that could provide an outstanding service. It should be understood that although some mediums work together, the vast majority are quite capable of taking the whole service alone.

As with any job or profession, the way in which the work is done is as important as doing the work. Especially so is the presentation of the work of a medium, whether giving a reading, giving an inspired talk or making a link with the spirit world for the demonstration of life continuous. Regardless of whether a medium works in trance or not, everything that is said, in law, is solely the responsibility of the medium. There are many times when loved ones, who wish to give a message to their nearest and dearest, use language that is colourful, and is unsuitable for uttering in a public place. Caution must be observed.

It is unfortunate, that with people who are unused to speaking in public, they tend to mutter and speak indistinctly, with no voice projection. When working for spirit the medium is their representative, and therefore if it is necessary, should have coaching on how to speak and project the voice. This may fly in the face of those who have regional accents, but as the object is to communicate, there is a responsibility on the medium to be able to talk to the audience so that they can understand fully, what is being said. It would be a shame if you were the recipient of a fantastic message, and you could not hear it, either because it was inaudible, slurred or even badly expressed. Another aspect with some mediums is the feeling that they are of a grander disposition than the other people who are gathered together. Arrogance is not a nice quality, nor is an affected voice. The main thing is to be normal, speak clearly and enunciate all the words.

There needs to be an understanding from audiences and congregations, that communication is very much like a telephone exchange. Spirit is the caller, the medium is the operator, and you are the one receiving the call. Think of a conversation with someone that you know very well. You know who it is, so no names are mentioned and because of the message, the recipient will know more than the 'telephone operator' does. I have said many times that unfortunately there are no circles to learn how to receive a message. We can, and do, teach all other aspects of spirit communication.

There are many different ways of being taught. It is quite surprising to walk into a church where we have not been before, and watch and listen to a medium that is new to us. Often, we have guessed correctly, at who the teacher was. For those taught by Gordon Higginson and his students, it is normal to hear a congregation spoken to with great respect, with clarity and with compassion. Conversely some students pick up some bad habits, such as finishing nearly each sentence with the word 'please'. As with any public speaking, care must be exercised. Repetition of words, causes an audience to start counting how many times a word is used, so that they lose interest in what is really going on.

Repetition can be seen in other ways, apart from the way in which we speak. It is normal for us to move our hands and arms, because that is the way we all communicate, but when a medium comes to the stage of giving a reasonable service or demonstration they should ask a friend to video it. Later, when viewing with a couple of friends, it may clearly show something that you did not know that you were doing. This gives you a chance to put things right before allowing a bad habit to really take hold. Nowadays, there are many 'teaching mediums' who produce clones of themselves, and their students portray the same stance, asides and gestures that they have been taught. Not always a pretty sight!

Bad language is never acceptable, and this can cause a medium real problems, because often spirit relatives can return using the same colourful language that they have always used. Therefore, all mediums have to be constantly aware of what is being said, and not to offend the sensibilities of the rest of the audience. I understand that when giving a demonstration, there is a certain degree of latitude given, but with a divine service that latitude is not even acceptable.

If we now look at the specifics of either a demonstration or service, we should start with the physical presentation of the church or centre. This may seem to be a basic requirement, but there are places that we have been to where expected standards were not in place.

The venue should be clean and tidy, with sufficient seating in reasonably comfortable chairs. There needs to be some sort of control over the ambient temperature. Trying to work (as we have) in a venue with no heating in the depth of winter tends to negate spirit connection. Whatever type of music is being played, it needs to be correct when married up with the words in the song book. Some places prefer hymns and some prefer up-to-date music with meaningful words. The choice sometimes dictates the audience. Additionally, the person controlling the music needs to be aware of what the job entails.

The chairperson is someone who has a very important job. They are not there just to make the number up. Apart from controlling the order of the service/demonstration, they are there to provide energy for the medium, to watch over the proceedings and to ensure that it is presented in the best way possible. There are times when a chairperson may have to stop the service/demonstration, such as if the medium's demeanour or language is unacceptable, or because some other problem has arisen. This means that the chairperson needs to be a strong person, with an understanding of how to provide energy for the medium and how to make the time spent at the venue as perfect as possible.

When the service/demonstration has been completed, the next job is to thank the medium on behalf of the church/centre (apart from the general thanks) and to ensure that they have a cup of tea and a biscuit. Even then it is not finished. There now needs to be the mediums fee, which should also be provided by the chairperson. This needs to be done tactfully. Last of all, there needs to be private or public thanks given to those that have made a contribution to the running of the church/centre. Being a chairperson is not just a fill-in job—it is very important, so much so that I have provided an evening class to teach just that job.

Part of the teaching of mediums must be how to provide a presence, how to clearly say what they want to in a clear and calm way. It is not a production of theatre work, so there is no need to act, just to be natural and do the job properly. This is an area where teachers/leaders really need to provide enough information for the betterment of mediumship as a whole.

One of the areas that is beginning to slip is the clothes that some mediums wear. I am fully aware that many people today wish to relax the standards, and to a certain extent I agree. Whenever my wife and I took a service we were always dressed smartly. If we take a pride in what we do, then why should we not take a pride in the way that we present ourselves? We are representatives of the spirit world. I have seen some mediums turning up to take a service in jeans and scruffy shirt. What people see in the first instance is how each person is judged, and quite often it may give an entirely false image.

People's voices are sometimes a difficulty. I find that a very broad accent is difficult to listen to, but I would not expect any false accent to replace it. I would much rather the speaker to slow down a little and speak a little more clearly. Many of us have regional accents and I, for one, would not like to see that changed. We are all different, and that is how it should be. There is a move to standardise the way in which we speak, but I would not like that to happen.

Microphones can be a big problem for some people; so a little practice at home can help. When you get to the venue, ask to try the sound level before the audience/congregation arrives. It could save some embarrassment. While on the subject of embarrassment, I know of one medium who was somewhat entranced, who took on the persona of the communicator. The communicator was a stripper. Luckily the performance did not go too far!

Anything that you are uncertain about, discuss it with the chairperson before taking the stage, including knowing what the format is. I have been to some churches where it seemed to be a bit of guesswork. Luckily, as we have had some experience, we were prepared for it and nobody knew the difference. My wife and I have also been in the position where there was no chairperson, so I had to do that job as well.

The overall approach to demonstrating, is that things can—and often do—go wrong. Preparation is the key. If the medium is at the venue in plenty of time, then they should make themselves aware of the situation in which they place themselves. If there is a microphone, is it working? Where the medium stands, can they be seen? Is the position at the right height, and if there is a lectern, is it in the way. Will there be a glass of water available? If there are notes, is there somewhere that they can be placed? Is there a copy of the proceedings so that the medium is aware of what is happening, and when?

In a theatre setting, does the lighting person know what they are doing? Does the back-of-stage staff know what is wanted? Whether you are the medium, the chairperson or organiser, the important thing is to check, check and then check again. If all eventualities are catered for, then there should be a more relaxed atmosphere, which allows better work.

So what is the best way of working?

There are many ways that mediums use. A quite common method is to give some random information and hope that someone 'bites'. A more advanced way is to generalise and say I'm somewhere over there, with a wave of the hand. Some try and give a description of the person in the spirit world who they think wants to communicate.

I have been in a room, where at a certain time the doors are locked, and seen a medium giving everyone a message. I have witnessed two mediums working together, one drawing and the other demonstrating. The picture will be accepted by one of the audience, and the other medium then homes in on them. The only problem was, that the first pieces of information were no accepted, but after about a minute, the information was accepted. What happened was, that there was a mix-up between the mediums, but then spirit sorted it out.

If we accept that there are spirit persons who have come to give a message, and that there is a spirit person (or more) for each person in the audience, then potentially there is a message for everyone. Each spirit person knows the person that they want to communicate with, so what is the problem? It is the medium!

If a medium is good enough, then they should be able to 'tune in' to the spirit person. If they can do that then what is the problem with asking the spirit person "What is your name and who is it that you wish to communicate with?".

How nice would it be if the medium said something like this: "I have got Jenny here who passed when she was 85, and she wants to talk to her daughter, Kate Duffy". All the messing about and lack of clarity would go. A sceptic would say that the rest of the audience would be lost, but in reality, the audience would be so 'gob-smacked' that they would really pay close attention. I have seen this happen.

Just think; clear information—not drawn out—would mean that the medium could give more contacts, and also the paying audience would be on-side as well. What a bonus! The only problem is which medium could do it. Who is willing to change their position from 'I'm fully developed' to 'I am still learning'. Quality is paramount. I would like to see mediums being much better than they are at present, and I hope that it happens before I leave this earth. Our forerunners, such as Gordon Higginson, etc. would be pleased if mediums achieved what they did, as a minimum.

A last note: when carrying out a demonstration, the audience will follow certain mediums, and therefore know quite a bit about 'their' medium. It seems that some mediums like to constantly provide information about their life, as opposed to giving a demonstration. Many times have I listened to mediums talking about themselves for a long time and then finish by giving five (5) messages. Not good enough, especially when a lot of money has changed hands and there are up to a few thousand people attending!.

CHAPTER 12

PRIVATE READINGS

SECTION 1 YOU, THE SEEKER.

First of all choose very carefully whether or not to have a private reading. Next decide whether your reason for a reading is to do with material things, such as relationship or money problems, or spiritual things, such as communication from loved ones. Then decide by asking others, who the best medium could be. It is not sensible to select a medium haphazardly, because that may not help you and could add to your problems. If you had a choice of going to a medium who never advertised, and was difficult to obtain a sitting with, as opposed to a medium who advertises every week and you can easily get an appointment, which would you choose? Common sense must always prevail.

Many people go to psychic fairs, and years ago they were excellent. The thought should be; should I pay a higher price for a reading for a shorter amount of time, especially when I have already paid an entrance fee. Add to that, the surroundings and ambient noise level are not very conducive to a balanced reading. How much better to be in comfortable surroundings, with maybe some mood music in the background and an attentive medium. A half way system could be used, where you go to a psychic fair and watch the mediums working. You can then pick up their business cards and see them at a later date in more conducive surroundings. Unfortunately, there are many money-making schemes going on, where the sitting for a person is less important than the money they will hand over. This is why it is important that the reading is given by a medium that comes highly recommended. Just because a medium has a well-known name or has a good piece of advertising does not guarantee a good, or even adequate, reading. This I have learned, to my cost.

SECTION 2 YOU, THE MEDIUM.

Over the years, mediumship was often carried out in the medium's kitchen or front room. Nowadays, hopefully, things are changing. My wife and I have a custom-built sanctuary that is used for all spiritual work. Over the years we have done readings, carried out hands-on and trance healing, run circles for development of healing, mediumship and transfiguration, and also have had physical phenomena. We also provided a course for chairpersons.

Where you as a medium work, will reflect on your total presentation. As with anything, quality must be paramount. Somewhere comfortable, even with a bit of professionalism in the surroundings helps to reassure the seeker. A table/desk with a nice tablecloth would also help. Whether you work as a spiritual medium, a card reader, palmist or numerologist, the principle is the same—just use complete professionalism.

Readings are not a friendly get-together for a laugh or a slip-shod way of making some money. It is a professional service that requires all the best that is within you to be shown. Often there is a need within a reading for some counselling to take place. Again, this needs to be done on a purely professional basis. If it seems that many of your readings contain some element of counselling, then it would be appropriate to go on a course and learn more about the subject, so that you come across as knowing how to advise and counsel your sitter.

Sometimes we are asked for opinions and guidance. We must, as professionals, be honest. If I do not know something, then I say so; but I then say I will find out and then let them know. Each medium, regardless of the stage that they are at in their development, must always strive to do better. Any medium who says *'I am fully developed and do not need to learn any more'* is under a massive delusion. Any medium worth their salt carries on learning until they leave this world. Nobody is perfect!

Whatever means that you use to give a reading, it can be polished more. For the tarot reader, why not use psychic perception of the sitter and the help of spirit to augment your card reading. It really works much better, and this can always be improved upon. Because most people require a mixture of spiritual contact and materialistic guidance, I have used this procedure for many years. My viewpoint is that anyone who comes to me needs all their boxes ticked, whether they are spiritual, material or just general questions. I do not want anyone leaving me with some questions unanswered. It is not professional.

With many of the best mediums there seems to be many problems in their lives. I often hear these mediums saying *'Why me?'* The answer is that unless we have experienced all the problems that we have had, then how can we possibly guide and help someone else? Many mediums have had relationship problems, money problems and health problems. They have got through it somehow, so the benefit of their experience comes into play when giving a reading/counselling sitting.

SECTION 3 PREPARING TO GIVE A READING.

Although it is perfectly possible to give a reading without preparation, it is much better to make time to prepare for the client. A clarification of the mind-set, getting rid of the daily worries and attention to the surroundings can greatly enhance a reading. In many cases there is a mind-blowing reaction where the recipient of the reading can have a complete change of life. It would not be reasonable to take matters lightly when this situation happens. Professionalism must be paramount.

First of all, the area that the sitting will take place must be clean and tidy. If you have a room put aside for this work, then ensure that it acceptable for anyone, regardless of who they are, to feel comfortable.

A comfortable (but not too comfortable) chair should be provided both for yourself and your client. Sometimes a table between you would be helpful, and this would certainly be so if you have somebody that you do not know, especially if you were female and the client was male.

This leads to who should your clients be. I know of some female mediums that will only give readings to females. If you could possibly feel vulnerable, then to have someone else within calling distance would help allay any of your fears. Most people are fine, but there are times when mentally disturbed people can request a sitting, and that is the time when you should be aware of what is going on. Anyone who either has an attitude problem, or seems to be mentally disturbed, should be turned away, using some excuse that seems plausible. Have a set situation in your mind for any possible refusal; whether someone has just arrived who needs you urgently, or that you have to go out. Just make sure that your excuse can hold water.

If you set aside a specific amount of time for your reading, then give enough time between readings so that you can relax for a little while. There are also times when your client needs a bit longer than the time that you have allocated, so that needs to be a consideration. Additionally, there may be times when you wish to just chat with the person after the sitting, and that will take time. Each individual is a real person not just a bringer of money, and they need to be treated as such. As a guide, a reading that takes about 40 to 45 minutes should cover all eventualities, and if a further 15 minutes is left before seeing someone else, then it gives time for a cup of coffee or a comfort break for the medium.

Costs are another consideration. What is it reasonable to charge? There are some mediums that feel that they are better than anyone else who charge phenomenal amounts of money. Often they are not as good as the quiet medium that does not charge a lot, but provides very good evidence. I have heard of mediums that charge well over £250 for an hour—or less. This does not mean that they are any better than anyone else, in fact as often as not they are only looking at the money side, and are not that interested in the client except as a provider of money. I have had readings from well-known mediums, and have been disappointed, whereas with a medium that charged an acceptable amount of money, I was pleased with the reading (and also the cost!).

As this is going to be a professional environment, there needs to be a word said about personal presentation. Clean, tidy and smart will provide the right presentation. Smoking also needs to be mentioned—not as a personal vendetta, but as a reasonable approach. In the 'old days' it was quite normal to have a reading with a medium that had a permanent cigarette in their mouth. Today, things have changed. It is unacceptable to give a reading in a smelly room, and that includes personal hygiene. If there has to be any smell (or aroma), then ensure that it is acceptable to the majority of people that you see.

Lighting needs to be at a reasonable level. Gone are the days when an oil lamp that was just giving enough light to see with. We are in a better age, and the amount of lights that are available is wide, so a gentle but bright enough light to be comfortable is fine. So, having set the scene, we move on towards the actual reading.

Preparation of self is important. Some mediums like to have half-an-hour linking in with spirit before a reading, others wish to relax and leave their worries and concerns behind, and some go through a meditation. Whatever you do is fine, provided that you condition yourself to the thought that you are going to do your very best for the person that you will be seeing, regardless of their hopes or problems.

A decision needs to be made as to whether or not to have more than one client at the same time. Generally, both my wife and I will only see one person at a time. This is because if there is a connection with the spirit world, then it could all be for one person and not the other. Often there is a lot of really personal information, and it would not be prudent to allow anyone else to hear it. Another decision is whether or not to allow a recording of the sitting. In general maybe not, because of the personal information that could be heard at a later date, by someone who really should not hear it. Sometimes on a recording, spirit will not allow a recording of part of a message. This has happened on a number of occasions in the past, where it sounds as though there were workmen close by making a very large noise, but in fact there was absolute quiet at the time of the recording.

When your client arrives, greet them in a friendly way with a smile. Let them be seated and get any pleasantries out of the way before you ask them how you can help them. Their problem can be generalised in the following ways: spiritual, material or their health. Having established what they require, make a quick assessment of what you are going to do. If you are concerned about time then have a small clock in front of you, and if you find that you cannot refer to it easily, have one with a gentle alarm or a timer. Set your time for 5 minutes short of that which you have provided, and that will give you 5 minutes to tie up any loose ends.

When dealing with health questions, then great care must be observed. The only person who, legally, is entitled to give a diagnosis is a qualified doctor. The mental awareness of the client makes a great deal of difference to what they think they hear, as opposed to what you actually said. An untrue concept can give rise to legal problems, so all that is said should be able to stand up in a court of law.

In general, although a person has come for a specific reading, it also helps if other aspects can be touched on. If someone has come for a material problem (which is most cases) then a contact with the spirit world can also be helpful. If it a purely spiritual reading, then a little spiritual guidance can also help.

At the end of the reading and during the last 5 minutes, ask if there are any further questions. Try and tie up any loose ends. If this is not possible, then tell the person that you will find out and will get back to them—and if you do say it, do it.

When you take your payment, ensure that you have any change that you might need so that there is no fiddling about looking for change. A small box out of sight is useful, but do not leave too much money in it for security reasons. If you receive a cheque, then ensure that it is correctly filled in, together with any security annotations. The client has given you their attention during the sitting, so it is prudent to give the cheque due attention. Give any last minute reassurances, and let them go with a smile—hopefully on both faces.

SECTION 4 TELEPHONE READINGS

This is not an area of work for all mediums. I have tried it and became bored very quickly. Apart from not having a face to look at, you could be doing anything that was distracting. You need to be fully aware of the reading as soon as the 'phone rings.

First of all, if working for a commercial group, there will be an expectance from them to provide a free reading so that you can be assessed. If you pass this stage, then you will be given all the necessary information to do the job. You will be asked to provide the times that you are willing to be available—and they could be a choice from anywhere within a 24 hour, 7 day a week slot. Some mediums like to work in the evening or at night, as there may be more callers then.

If you are really flexible, you can do your household chores while waiting for the telephone to ring. You will probably be selected in turn by a computer. If you miss your call (maybe by going to the toilet), you will miss your turn and have to wait for the next turn. You have to keep records of what you do, with whom and when. If the computer is on a modern system, the recording of the messages will be done for you, but if not, you have to do your own recording and then send the tape to the correct address of the caller.

It helps if you have a headset, so that you can walk around (so as to not miss your call), but whatever you are doing, you need to stop within about three rings and do the reading. I found that the biggest problem was that the callers that I had, were in the main women wanting information on their relationships, and wanted someone to tell them what to do. I believe that we are solely responsible for all that we do, and although at times we need a bit of guidance, we should not ask someone else to sort out our lives as an ongoing job. If you feel that this is an area of work for you, then you have my good wishes.

CHAPTER 13

HEALING

Currently, there is a two-year national course run by various organisations, under the banner of the UK Healers. This was regularised and the name adopted in August 2001. The UK Healers has established both a Code of Conduct and Complaints and Disciplinary Procedures that apply to all healer members. These standards are to protect the public when they receive healing from a healer registered with UK Healers (a UK Registered Healer). UK healers are required to be properly insured as a condition of registration.

A brochure is obtainable from UK Healers setting out their parameters of healing. They can be contacted at: PO Box 4137, London W1A 6FE. Their website is on: www.ukhealers.info

Healers, which is a bit of a misnomer, are people who act as a medium where the actual healing comes from a spiritual source. There are some people who do 'magnetic' healing, but in the main healers provide the contact between the patient and the spirit source. They provide either hands-on or distant healing. They are not allowed to provide clairvoyance, clairaudience or clairsentience during a healing session. It is generally accepted that our friends in the spirit world do specialise, so if we work with a doctor, we have to change guides to provide clairvoyance, except in special cases.

I am a healer and healer trainer and have been on an assessment panel to find out if those who have been trained are up to the standard required by UK Healers. I have taken the basic information from the standard set by the United Spiritualists, of which I am a member.

Essentially, there are four modules, each taking 6 months to complete. During the two years, there has to be 200 hours of recorded healing supervised by the trainer as an additional requirement. The reason that the course is organised over this period of time is to ensure (as far as possible) that those who are being trained will demonstrate their commitment and abilities.

Before starting the course, there is a need to become a member of the organisation that is training you. Apart from the yearly fee, there is also a separate fee for insurance. A trainee currently pays a total of about £21 (including insurance). Once you have passed the course and become a full healer member the cost (including insurance) is the same. Once accepted, you should be issued with an identity card.

There are a few questions that need to be asked prior to the acceptance for the course and commencement of the course. These questions are:

Have you ever been refused a membership of any organisation?

Are there any circumstances that may affect your application, such as a criminal record or a chronic health problem?

Followed by a declaration that the above statements are true and that you agree to abide by the rules of the organisation to which you are applying.

A code of practice is used giving guidelines on how things should be carried out. There is also a disciplinary procedure in case things are done wrongly, mostly to do with common sense. The reason is to ensure that the high standards, which have been set by others, are maintained. Healers are not allowed (by law) to diagnose illnesses. A qualified doctor can only do this. Each healer trainer has learned their vocation, and has been approved to teach.

There are certain aspects of the law that trainees must be aware of, including access to medical reports, access to health records, data protection and police and criminal evidence. Ignorance is not an acceptable plea. When giving healing to children there is a need to ensure that they are of a certain age. If they are below 16 years old (UK), then it is part of the procedure to request a written consent from the child's parent or guardian.

A broad statement is do not do anything (including anything to do with dentistry and prescribing ANY medicines, remedies, herbs, etc) unless you are qualified to do so. Notifiable diseases, midwifery and sexually transmitted diseases also have restrictions.

With regard to animals, healing may be given, but no diagnosis may be made except by a veterinary surgeon, and no other treatment is permissible.

Each module is a complete study containing much information. At the end of the module is a questionnaire that has to be completed before moving on to the next module, and that will only be at the end of the six-month period. A Code of Conduct is part of the study so that each trainee will understand the parameters in which to work.

When all modules have been completed including answering all the questions and with sufficient supervised healing, a reference from three independent patients, during the two years that it takes to complete the course, you would be examined by an assessment panel of healers. The panel normally comprises three healers, one of which may be the teacher of the trainees.

Module 1

This contains the preparation of a trainee together with practical and theoretical information. Each of the Chakras is explained in a basic way, together with the position and colour that is associated with each one. It also includes the practical approach to meeting people who require healing and how to treat them. How to open and close chakras is also explained.

Each step of the way is clearly and sensibly presented. One of the first things to be aware of is the confidentiality of the healing as there are rules imposed by doing this sort of work. Unless required by law, nothing must be divulged to anyone at any time. Although the Hippocratic Oath is not normally used by any other person except doctors, it **is** used by healers.

HIPPOCRATIC OATH

The regimen I adopt shall be for the benefit of my patients according to my ability and judgement, and not for their hurt or for any wrong. I will give no deadly drug to any though it be asked of me, nor will I counsel such, and especially will not aid a woman to procure abortion.

Whatsoever house I enter, there I will go for the benefit of the sick, refraining from all wrong-doing or corruption, and especially from any act of seduction, of male or female, of bond or free.

Whatsoever thing I see or hear, concerning the life of men, in my attendance on the sick or even apart therefrom, which ought not to be noised abroad, I will keep silence thereon.

Next comes the introduction to healing and it's historical background. Most people are aware that Jesus was a great healer, apart from being a wonderful medium, and usually that is where the history starts. Some historians suggest that as there was use of herbs and other concoctions, that healing started way before Jesus. Royalty practised healing in the England in the 1400's by Henry 7th, and in France in the 1600's by Louis 14th.

A few years ago, a clinical trial was held in America with regard to healing. A small surgical incision was made on the arms of 40 people. Half the people were given healing and the remainder were left to heal naturally. There was no understanding by the people as to who had healing and who did not. Those who had healing healed faster than those who did not.

Healing is often equated to energy. Because there is no scientific proof, opinions vary. Theories, such as that held by Mesmer, include magnetic healing, some think that the source is from the earth energy; while others think that the energy either comes from the healer or from some heavenly source. Whatever it is, it works.

The usual way of explaining how healing actually works is that the healer 'channels' the energy (from whatever source) through themselves to the patient. As with anything, ability is a variable, as each of us is capable of healing, but some are better than others. There is also a viewpoint (which I subscribe to) that some people who cannot be healed by one person, can be by another.

Healing is not a universal panacea, but can help many people. It is also not a cure-all, as some patients die. In this case, healing can help a person to pass away in a much more comfortable way, and maybe with less pain. It must be said that normal treatment by a doctor should always be continued. Healers are not doctors, and cannot replace them. A healer must work with others who have the patients' interest at heart and have a qualification to do so. There is some move by traditional doctors towards the use of healing, so any helpful way of working with them would be reasonable.

In the 'old days' it was quite natural to see healers waving their arms about. This process is now not accepted. It does not benefit the patient if you frighten them, especially if they are frail and old or children. Equally, there is no need to breathe in a disturbing fashion. When giving healing to non-Christians, and if you have a Christian bias, do not insult them by using the sign of the cross as some do.

Any healer worth their salt would never give an undertaking to be able to cure any illness. Any healer that does, I would keep well away from, as they are guaranteeing something that they cannot do.

Healing can be applied to the following conditions, apart from those that are obvious: stress, guilt, anger and any other negative aspects. Again—no guarantees. Sometimes the patient only wants to talk. This also is a form of healing, although I would suggest that a counsellor's course might help the healer in such cases. Another aspect, which must be observed, is that if the healer is unwell they should not give healing until they are well again.

There are a number of basic points that need to be covered before actually getting in to the healing itself. Reliability, discipline and commitment with cleanliness both in self and clothes need addressing. If you smoke or drink alcohol, there needs to be no smell of either. Some healers wear a white coat similar to doctors, but although there needs to be cleanliness, normal clean clothes are more than acceptable. There is no need to try and copy being a doctor, because we are not. Washing hands between patients is how some healers work, but others do not. There may be a situation where you would normally not wash your hands, and then your next patient is smelly. The easiest way around that would be to heal through the aura and not to actually touch them. Diplomacy is paramount. Providing healing to people who have either open wounds or transmittable diseases needed to be decided before the situation occurs. Common sense prevails.

Attunement to the healing energy will allow you to develop more quickly. This is usually done through meditation. Meditation is the cornerstone of spiritual progression and should not be dismissed as being a waste of time. It is accepted that meditation will help balance the mind, body and spirit.

Elsewhere in this book (in Chapter 8) there are a number of meditations. Essentially, sitting on an upright chair in the Egyptian meditation position, with calming music in a peaceful area will do much to enhance your meditation. 10 minutes a day can work wonders, and if you add absent healing you will be helping others at the same time. It really does help if you sit with other like-minded people.

Because it is important to do things correctly, there should be a system of keeping records of patients. It is possible that in a healing group, which offers healing to others, that the same healer may not be available, therefore the records will allow continuity.

Prior to the start of any healing, it is usual with many healers to offer a silent prayer and open your chakras. The prayer includes a request for protection both for yourself and for anyone to whom you give healing. It also is the time to ask for their help to be given to the people that you will see. Some healers also open the chakras of the patient immediately prior to the commencement of healing.

Potential patients may not know what to expect from healing, so it may need explaining. This is the first part of ensuring that the patient is comfortable. Your approach and first words are what the patient is aware, and it does not help to frighten them, especially as there is really nothing that can harm them. Some people have preconceived ideas that may be totally erroneous. If a child requires healing, the parental permission form must be completed and signed before any healing is started. Diagnosis is acceptable within our own minds, but we are not allowed to give the diagnosis to the patient. This is only permissible if you are a doctor.

Before I start any healing—and especially with the opposite sex—I state where my hands will **not** go. It may sound strange, but if your patient is new to healing and they do not really know what will happen, their mind will work overtime to try and think what will happen, usually in a negative way. Next, I ask how I can help. Having obtained the answer, I then stand behind them and put my hands on their shoulders. This (for me) does two things. I make a contact with the patient and also orientate myself to the patient. The orientation allows me to be aware in my own body where there is a problem with the patient, and if I am looking the same way as the patient, my left is their left and so on. So if I am aware of pain in my right leg, then the patient has a pain in their right leg. Not all healers work in this way.

Healers, according to their insurance, are not allowed to do anything except the laying on of hands. This means that healers are not allowed to massage unless they have a relevant qualification, but even in this context it is unacceptable to give healing and massage at the same time.

A lot of information is available with regard to doing the actual healing and this can be split into two areas. One is to maintain a contact on the shoulders and the other is to place the hands on the area that requires healing. The second situation can be a little delicate if giving healing to the opposite sex—and sometimes to the same sex—as no touching is allowed in areas where it could be construed as being inappropriate. In this situation, I advise healing through the aura, and that does not mean being 'nearly touching'.

When the healing is completed for a patient, then as you have opened their chakras, you must close them. When you have totally completed your healing then your chakras must be closed also. To finish off, it is courteous to say a 'thank you' prayer to your spirit friends.

Before your patient leaves you, ensure that they are comfortable with the healing and answer any questions. It may be that they will require further treatment, as with several healing applications, the healing becomes more effective. Last of all complete your records. Remember that you are providing a service and that the quality that you provide reflects on all healers. Being professional is paramount. Having a chat is not appropriate while healing, but can happen when the healing has been completed.

MODULE 2

When giving healing, there may be environmental problems, and these need to be reduced where possible. Apart from your own concentration, it is disturbing for the patient, so whatever you can do to alleviate the problem will be beneficial. This includes how you are feeling at the time of giving healing. If you have just had a passionate argument immediately prior to giving healing, it will reduce the efficacy of that healing, and may not help the patient at all. It may even pass on your anger to them—which is the last thing that is wanted.

To feel extra aches and pains to that which you normally have may indicate that these are the pains of the patient. This is not for you to tell the patient, but to pass on to your spirit guide. You are only the person who is the intermediate between the spirit world and the patient. That is to say you are the channel for the healing process to pass through. There are benefits from this, as all healing which passes through you, some is left with you and therefore you do have healing too! It is unacceptable to retain the symptoms that you have picked up from your patient. There is a theory that it is because you have not passed the information on to the spirit guide, but if you feel that you have, there will come a time when they will fade, and then only be present during the time that the information is given.

Within this module is information about the human aura. All living things have an aura, and this has been demonstrated by Kirlian photography. Some mediums can see the human aura, but many cannot. The aura can be 'felt' by two people bringing a hand close to the other person's. By gently moving the hands around two to six inches from each other a sensation can be felt. This is the aura, but depending upon the sensitivity of an individual, the aura can be expanded to a large degree. Someone who can see auras as a brownish colour can sometimes perceive unwellness (as opposed to illness). Brighter colours can indicate the spirituality of the person.

When there is a feeling that someone is invading your space it is possibly because your auras are in close proximity. There is a line of thinking that there are a number of bodies that emanate in layers from our physical body. The one next to the physical body is the etheric body, the next is the spiritual body, and then one to do with our mental processes and the fourth is our astral body.

The chakras are explained in more detail. There are many chakras throughout our body, but the main ones are the seven in our body and one in each of our hands. Chakra is a Sanskrit word which means wheel. Looking at a chakra chart, it shows each chakra as a spinning vortex that can be likened to a wheel. Each chakra contra-rotates to the next one. The base chakra is located at the base of the spine and is sometimes referred to as the Kundalini, with an associated colour of red. The next, moving upwards, is the sacral and is located 2 inches below the navel, with an associated colour of orange. The next is the solar plexus with the colour of yellow. Next is the heart chakra with the colour of green. These constitute the lower chakras. The first of the upper chakras is located at the throat, with the colour of pale blue. Next is the forehead, with the colour of indigo. Lastly is the crown chakra with violet (although sometimes the colours silver or gold are used).

Opening a chakra is done by visualising either a bud opening or (as I teach) unlocking a door and then opening it wide. Opening is usually going up through the chakras and closing is going down (open up and close down). Closing is either closing a bud or shutting a door and locking it. The choice is yours and what you feel comfortable in doing. There are many books that give information on the activation of the chakras and how to keep them clear and functioning well, so it is a good idea to do more research and polish the knowledge that you have.

Absent healing is also covered. The great healer, Harry Edwards, said that absent healing is more efficacious than contact healing. All absent healing requires is a quiet place, an attunement with spirit and the offering of names for healing in an unrushed way. A prayer to start and finish with is also helpful. Obviously it is sensible to keep in contact with those for whom absent healing has been asked for, just to ensure that it has been helpful and that you are interested in the well-being of the patient. Absent healing can be done either by one person or as a group.

MODULE 3

This covers the physical aspects of healing. Although many organisations previously did nothing with regard to gaining knowledge of the human anatomy, this has now changed, and there is now a requirement to have a reasonable understanding. One of the viewpoints is, if a patient repeats what a doctor has told them, and then there is a greater possibility of a better understanding of the patient's complaint or illness.

The systems that are covered are the cardio-vascular, respiratory, digestive, excretory, nervous, hormonal, skeletal, muscular, lymph-vascular and the reproductive systems of males and females. Further reading should take place in medical books, as this is only a layman's guide.

CARDIO-VASCULAR SYSTEM

The structure of the heart is taught, together with how the heart makes the blood flow through the body. The pumping of the blood depends on various responses and these functions are illustrated. The plasma is also discussed. Many people, who do not know anything about the body, understand what stress is and what happens to people who suffer from it. Stress impacts on the heart, causing many problems; therefore we all need to be aware of the result of stress and how to manage it.

RESPIRATORY SYSTEM

The lungs are the main element of the respiratory system, and with the constant advertising against smoking, more and more people are becoming aware of how the lungs work (or not, as the case may be). The lungs are not equal in size. The right lung is shorter than the left (because the diaphragm rises higher on the right to accommodate the liver) although it is larger.

DIGESTIVE SYSTEM

We are all aware that eating is the main entrance to the digestive system, and some of us know that what we put into our mouths makes a difference to how our bodies function. The food that we eat goes into the digestive system after being broken down in part by chewing. The food then enters the small intestine where it is broken down further and the nutrients are absorbed into the blood supply. The waste products are then moved into the large intestine and then excreted. The liver processes the products of the digestion that have been absorbed passing into the blood stream.

NERVOUS SYSTEM

This is the body's communication system that is controlled by the brain. Because each of us is different, we react to various stimuli differently;

this is what makes us individuals in this context. There are a number of different nervous systems within the system as a whole. Many have heard of the sciatic nerve, but there are others, which include the tibial, peroneal, saphenous, lumbar-sacral plexus, lumbar plexus, radial, median, ulnar, intercostal, brachial plexus, spinal cord and cerebral cortex.

Hormonal system

Simply put, hormones are switches. They switch on or off certain processes in the cells of our body, which can make a large change in the way our body cells function, despite the fact that there are only a very small amounts in the bloodstream.

Skeletal system

The adult skeleton consists of 206 bones, 26 of which are in the spine. Children have 33. The main bones are the skull, clavicle, sternum, humerus, radius, ulna, pelvis, sacrum, coccyx, femur, patella, fibula and tibia. We have 12 pairs of ribs, 11 of which are attached to the sternum. The lower pair are known as floating ribs.

Muscular system

Muscles account for about 50% of our weight (in an average person), and are to be found throughout the body. Wherever they are, muscles are constructed in the same way. Each muscle is made up from hundreds of elongated fibres. Each fibre is made up from thousands of fibrils, bound together in bundles by a membrane, through which nutrients and waste products can pass. Near the end of the muscle the tissues become denser, forming white cords, known as tendons, which are attached to bones. Muscles are made of three types; voluntary, involuntary and mixed.

Lymphatic system

This is a set of connecting channels, with relay stations, to ensure that immune cells are produced in large numbers and then poured into the bloodstream to combat infection. The lymphatic system runs parallel to the bloodstream and contains lymph nodes, which sense and react to infections. Our immune system is very complicated. It protects us from attack by organisms, fungus infections, bacteria and viruses.

Eating disorders

There is so much written about eating disorders that there is no reason to delve too deeply into this subject. Suffice to say, that there are three different types: compulsive eating, anorexia nervosa and bulima. The common factor in these disorders is the abnormal amount of food intake as well as an obsessive interest in food. The compulsive eater binges and grows fat; the anorexic deliberately starves themselves to keep thin (and is in danger of being emaciated); the bulemic binges and then either forces vomiting or uses laxatives in excess. Although healing may help—and this is more to do with mental changes, the important thing is to seek professional help from a doctor.

Diagnosis

Many healers can diagnose complaints and illnesses, but there is a danger that some information can be wrong at times. This is the reason that no proper healing course will allow trainees or even certificated healers to diagnose. Doctors are the only people who are allowed to diagnose, by law. This does not mean to say that diagnosis never takes place. I use diagnosis in the healing that I do, but I do not allow the patient to know the information that I get. Wrong information can have a huge impact on the patient, and is not ethical. It is quite acceptable, if you as a healer become very concerned for a patient to urge them to go to a doctor, but do not provide any diagnosis. A simple 'I would feel happier if you also saw a doctor as well as receiving healing' should be the approach.

In a different situation, I knew of a professional medium that used to tell married females that their husband would be dead in a few weeks. Because it did not happen, two ladies ended up having a complete breakdown. This is an instance of wrong information being given by someone who should have known better. Others who did not suffer a breakdown had to have all the negative aspects cleared and to be reassured by another medium, that was more in tune with the way the work should be done.

Other forms of healing

There are other ways of helping people who are unwell. These include counselling, crystal healing, aromatherapy, acupuncture, reflexology, osteopathy, chiropractic, homeopathy, hypnotherapy, colour treatment and regression. Each of these forms of healing should only be practised if you have a qualification to do them. None of these treatments should be 'tried' by anyone who has not been taught properly.

Counselling

This is an area fraught with stumbling blocks. Even an experienced counsellor can get into problems, as the patient can have vastly changing attitudes. Generally, counselling is not telling a person what to do, even if that is the logical approach. It mostly consists of listening and then feeding back the information, maybe in a slightly different way. Put simply, the object of the exercise is to allow the person who is receiving counselling, to understand their problem and to realise what they should do.

Crystal healing

There are many people who use crystal healing, and there seems to be some benefit from the crystals. The theory is that the crystals are used as an amplifier for the healing energy. It is a scientific fact that crystals vibrate at certain frequencies, and are used commercially. In practice, many people have had benefit.

Aromatherapy

This is mostly used with massage, and can have quite dramatic results. The main problem with massage is that areas of the body may be touched, and care must be taken not to step over the bounds of common decency. Carrier oils, which should be of top quality, are usually almond, soya, grape seed, avocado, peach and wheat germ, and are used with added essences. There are many aspects to aromatherapy, including how dilute the carrier oil, because of the body's ability to absorb it in different parts of the body. The actual massage can vary in pressure and direction. Certificated and competent people should only carry out aromatherapy.

ACUPUNCTURE

This is the traditional Chinese form of inserting very fine needles into the skin of the body. Their insertion is based on the concept of where the meridians are to be found, which carries the flow of energy (chi) throughout the body. The needles are to unblock points where the energy does not flow, allowing the body to recover from whatever dis-ease was prevalent. Certificated and competent people should only carry out acupuncture. Accupressure is similar to acupuncture, except that needles are not used, but the fingers and thumbs provide the stimulation on the surface of the skin.

REFLEXOLOGY

This follows the principles of acupuncture, except that it uses massage of the foot (usual) or hands to treat the body. There are many books on the subject, but I would advise taking a course, to learn properly from someone who is properly qualified to teach.

OSTEOPATHY AND CHIROPRACTIC

These are specialised treatments, and require much study by a recognised school. As this is not a subject that most healers come up against, it is left to the reader to find out what the various schools have to offer. Certificated and competent people should only carry out these treatments.

HOMEOPATHY

A homeopathic doctor carries out the treatment using different remedies from standard drugs. As I understand it some general practitioners go on to learn about the homeopathic process, and when qualified, may then practise.

Colour

The colour therapist usually floods the body (externally) with various colours, depending on the type of ailment. This works on the physical, emotional, mental and spiritual levels to balance the energies within the body, thereby restoring health and well-being. What we wear on a day-to-day basis is dependant (mostly) by our mood, at least when we have a choice. If we take that theory, then what we wear may change our inner selves to something different. I have always liked (and wear) very bright clothes, and maybe that is my personality and why I feel good most of the time.

Regression

Regression is an aspect of hypnotherapy, and is to do with taking the patient back to a former time in their life. It may be possible to determine any underlying triggers that have caused specific problems to the patient. Once the cause of the problem is determined, then a possible solution may be found. Additionally, regression can be used to determine past lives, but unless the person conducting the regression has a great deal of experience, it may just be for 'entertainment'.

MODULE 4

This is a good time to determine just how you are going to carry out your healing. Will you belong to a church, a group or set up on your own? If you are setting up on your own, then you should remain in close contact with your trainer. Should you wish to become a Healer/ Counsellor, you ought to consider working for a couple of years as a healer and then take a counsellor course. You may wish to give healing in hospitals, but for this you need to ask the hospital authorities if they will first give you permission, and even then there may be restrictions. I have found that just holding someone's hand—which is a natural thing to do in a hospital—provides a suitable healing connection.

Regardless of how you provide healing, you will need either a booking or waiting system, a waiting area, a treatment area and a means for recording information about your patient(s). There are many aspects that you have to consider. All of these are covered in the module. The important (and legal) implications must be observed. Keeping records generally covers these, and if there was a situation where you are being sued, you will need your records. You will also need your insurance.

What you need to record, and a simple record card indexed system will suffice, is the following: the patient's name, address, telephone number, date of the visit together with any comments, and in the case of children, a parent's signature, and the owner's signature when animals are being treated. The signature of the healer is also required as where there are other healers, there is a need to know who provided the healing on which date.

There are risks from your patients. You may be doing everything that is correct and proper, but that does not save you from someone who has a perception that you have done something wrong, or indeed, from someone who is against what you do and is making mischief. This is why many healers work together for protection.

The last areas are psychic surgery (more properly called spiritual surgery) and trance healing. These are not covered by insurance and neither is massage. Psychic surgery and trance, in law, are treated as though you are in full possession of all your faculties. In other words, saying that you are entranced by someone in spirit has no meaning in law, and that you are regarded as being totally responsible for all of your actions. Trainees are only covered by insurance during their training if they are being supervised.

I have seen many wonderful healings, including a young girl who was profoundly deaf beginning to hear. I have witnessed, close up, both psychic surgery on myself for worn out shoulders, and a woman who had a grapefruit sized fibroid shrunk to the size of a pea (with x-rays to prove it). There are so many healings, but the thing to remember is that one should not expect healing to take place perfectly every time. I also know of people who have experienced healing, and the condition was not helped. Sometimes it is to enable patients to put up with their problem, and sometimes it is help to give release from this world.

One man who was very sceptical of what we do eventually took up our offer of healing because he was in so much pain. He had MS, was laid off work and was confined to a wheelchair. He lived opposite us. One day he 'phoned and asked for help. He came over the road in his wheelchair, and we helped him to get into our house then sat him on a stool. This happened twice a week. Eventually he walked over to our house, went upstairs to our sanctuary (a large bedroom) two stairs at a time! He became fitter and eventually discarded his wheelchair and went back to work. He did eventually die some years later, but as a result of cancer and not MS.

Self-healing is an aspect that is widely encountered. It is a shame, because it does work. It only takes a little application. Essentially, our body heals itself, but there are times when an illness persists. Surprisingly, whatever is wrong with us can be directly related to our own concerns that we are choosing to inhibit. Our conditions can be associated with what is going on around us. For instance: if we keep rubbing our eyes, causing us to close our eyes, maybe we do not want to see what is either happening to us or is happening around us. With shoulder and back pains, it may be that we are taking on too heavy a load, or even taking on board someone else's load (or problem).

Those that give healing know that often healing is carried out through the aura, because this is where the initial awareness of illness is located. Subsequently, the illness will be apparent in the body. It is then not unreasonable to assume that we can heal ourselves through the aura. If we analyse ourselves and take time over it, then we should be able to determine if there is an imminent illness that has not yet shown itself in the body. By association, we can determine the prime cause of the oncoming problem. Once we understand how our body works, we are moving to the point where we could be problem free.

There is a theory that we should tune into our bodies and find out what we are doing, right or wrong. I heartily commend this procedure to everyone. Illness is an imbalance, and as such needs investigation by ourselves to see if we can put right the imbalance. When I see my doctor, I always ask how can I help myself. I am conscious that I do things incorrectly for my body, and then pay the price at a later stage. Unfortunately, I fall into the category of being either lazy or having too much to do. These are only excuses. I have the physical and mental ability to understand myself, and what makes me 'tick'. When I have done more research, I will hopefully update this book.

In the meantime, each of us can sit down and ask for our friends in the spirit world to take away our pain. All that we need to do is dedicate some time to do just that. Remember that it is courteous to thank them afterwards, and then not to do anything to jeopardise the situation again.

CHAPTER 14

FOLLOW-UP WORK

INTRODUCTION

This is an area where little has been done. Most mediums get to a point in their lives where they think that they have become 'developed'. I have news for them. They never become fully developed in this life. If they are doing their job correctly, they will tell you that they are still learning. I will freely admit that even after 50-odd years, I do not know everything with regard to mediumship, and I am still learning. I also have a philosophy, which says that I must pass on all the information that I have acquired in this life for the benefit of others, and that does not necessarily mean that I have to have money for what I do.

All too often I come across mediums that start off their mediumship with: 'I don't know who I'm with, but here is the information that I have got'. One medium that I have had the pleasure of seeing was Peter Geekie, from London, who worked at our centre. A member of the audience tried to claim the message, and he said that he had been doing his mediumship long enough to know who he was giving the message to. For him I have respect.

There have been enough instances for me to be certain that if the medium makes a decision to whom he/she is going, spirit will follow.

A well-known couple that I have witnessed many times proved the point for me. The man drew a likeness of someone in the spirit world. The picture was shown to the audience by the lady, and was then claimed. The lady then started her mediumship, most of which was not claimed. A change happened, and all that she next said *was* claimed. The understanding was, that the lady had picked up on a spirit person, but the wrong one to start with. Eventually the right communicator arrived and the message was correct.

I have maintained that when demonstrating mediumship, that the medium goes directly to the recipient. Provided sufficient application has been made with training, spirit friends will be working with the medium on the correct wavelength. Hoping that it will work by guessing where you are is not good enough. I have been to demonstrations long ago, where the door was locked and everyone in the audience had a message. Spirit must know what they are doing. We often do not, and most of it is down to a lack of professional training. As an analogy, we can all become carpenters, but we cannot all become cabinet makers without the correct tuition. The good bit is that we can all keep improving until we are the best that we can be.

The most important thing that we can do as mediums is to keep improving what we have got, and not only that, be prepared to change how we communicate the information that spirit gives us. The best mediums that I know will say to me that they did not think their communication was good enough, even when I knew that it was excellent. They demonstrate the fact that they are never satisfied with what they do and will keep striving to become a better instrument.

Many mediums fall into the trap of using (unconsciously) idiosyncrasies. These take the form of repetitive words such as 'please' at the end of nearly every sentence, or using other phrases such as 'do you understand'. While some words are quite acceptable, the repetitiveness causes the listeners to miss what is being said, because they are counting how many words or phrases are repeated.

When a medium, who is competent, is demonstrating; the audience is so engrossed in the quality of evidence that any small repetitiveness is glossed over and ignored. This is the standard that should be achieved by any good medium. Unfortunately, with some 'well-known' mediums, they are content to give half a dozen 'messages' and then spend time talking about their prowess. This denigrates the whole spiritual movement, and then we wonder why others say that it is just a moneymaking ploy.

Although many mediums will indicate that they are the representatives of spirit, often the understanding behind it is ignored. My interpretation is that we should be clean, smart and presentable, speak properly (regional accents are fine) and clearly, so that all the audience/congregation can hear and understand us. Add to that the quality of evidence needs to be impeccable, and then there is a fair chance that you will have an attentive audience. Unfortunately, some of the audience will be deaf to a certain degree—for whatever reason—while others will have a need to discuss something that has nothing to do with the demonstration. These are stumbling blocks and need to be understood and then planned for, prior to standing on platform.

To compensate for the deaf (ish), you may need a microphone or a more projected voice. To bring the focus of attention back to the evening for those who have got their own discussion group requires tact. A gruff put-down is not helpful for those that are on your side, as they will then be alienated, so each of us requires some thought on how to handle any given situation. Humour—but not sarcastic humour—will usually smooth over problems. What should be the target, is a demonstration where all the people want more, and not only that, they want to come to your next demonstration, bringing with them, their friends.

The other main aspect of a demonstration is to decide whether the time is spent as a spiritual connection, a psychic demonstration or a mixture of both. The set up should be decided before the event and advertised accordingly. Having made the decision, then that which is advertised must be how the time is spent. If it is a service, then a spiritual demonstration should be given, because what is expected is proof of survival. Too many times have I witnessed a service where the medium talks about where objects are located in the recipient's house, or other psychic 'evidence'.

As professional mediums, we should distance ourselves from the 'end of the pier' fortune telling. I have no problem with fortune-tellers, as they advertise themselves as such and provide a service to those that want it. My wife visited a fortune-teller at Brighton, just for interest. As the fortune-teller started to speak, my wife interrupted her with some spiritual evidence, providing some surprise. Yes, my wife was accurate!

Another time, we were on holiday and we saw a 'gypsy caravan' at a seaside resort. It was a man who is very well-known in the West Country. Again, just for interest, my wife went in. We were both in our holiday clothes, which were nondescript. When she eventually emerged after being inside for about four times the length everyone else had, she told me what had happened.

The man had asked her to hold a crystal ball, and then told her that she was a clairvoyant who worked on a far higher level than he did. He then went on to say that she was a healer (true). Some discussion followed, and before she left the caravan, he invited her to have a caravan and work next to him at a very popular venue in Somerset, England. Here was a man who knew the difference between being a 'proper' medium and a person who is an 'end-of-the-pier' worker. If only others could understand the difference!

Some mediums, including both my wife and myself find that we have a need to sit in a circle that is run by someone else from time-to-time. The reason being that we do not always want to be the leader, which is certainly a different aspect than just being guided. Each circle leader is different, and we need to keep polishing our skills, so to sit with another medium and be guided by them can only provide us with more facets of what we want to learn. It is also nice to communicate with spirit on a learning aspect rather than on a teaching aspect. It is also nice to be pushed to try and do our mediumship in different ways.

One of the most difficult things to do is to communicate with all people at all the different levels. Some of these are problems with vocabulary, some accents, some is just a basic understanding. Our job as a medium is to impart information from spirit to the person who is getting the message. If we cannot provide the information to the recipient because of a problem, then it is up to us to find a way around the problem. This may just be a case of rewording that which has been said. I have no problem with any medium that repeats the information in a different way for clarification.

Each of us is only as good as the last message that we have given. By doing the job right a few times does not mean that we can sit back and say that we can do it and do not need to keep learning and practising. Each message is a challenge that must be done to the best of our ability. It does not mean that we should not keep trying to improve.

The best way that I know of how to improve ourselves is to ask a friend to use a camcorder and make a recording of a demonstration that we do. Back at home, within a relaxed atmosphere; you can look with your own criticism at what you had done. As you watch, note all the problems that you think are there. Better still; ask a couple of friends to have a look also. If all the errors are rectified, then you are on your way to becoming a better medium. If you know any mediums, whose work you respect, ask them for some input with regards to your work. We are all in the learning process. There is no dishonour in asking for practical help and advice.

THE MIND

We all have one, but very few are able to use it completely. I know that the mind is the most important tool that we, as humans, have. Unfortunately there are few ways of reaching our potential on our own. It may be that the Internet will provide some exercises, but here are a few of my own. They may take some time to come to fruition, but as you all know, nothing comes without effort!

We all know that hands-on healing is initiated by thought, so the concept of sending a thought to make something happen is not a new one. Absent healing is also initiated in the same way. Maybe we also 'tune in'. You know that we can do it. Your mind, as I have said before, is the most powerful tool that you have. So, why not use it more towards its capacity?

Send a thought message for someone that you know to 'phone you. Choose that person; don't just think of 'anyone'. Be more specific. You are limited to the amount of time that you have to spare, so send a thought for the time that you want the 'phone to ring. Pushing things a little more, choose the subject that you will discuss.

You are visiting someone's home and you feel thirsty and then send out a thought for the host to offer you a drink. As a game, when the weather is fine and there are a few clouds in the sky, use your thoughts to break them up bit by bit, so that they dissipate. Having done some experimenting, and understanding some of the capacity of your mind, why not move on to how your mediumship works.

Many mediums suffer from nerves when carrying out a service or demonstration. Although it is very common—and most good mediums that I know have the problem—some of the nervousness is necessary to lift the adrenalin. If there is too much nervousness, then some form of help is required, which is why I have provided this information.

The most important aspect is to engage the mind to overcome disabilities. The disabilities to which I refer are a lack of confidence in all sorts of situations, overcoming panic attacks and many other mind problems. All of these are experiments. They are not end products that *will* happen, but *may* help you in your desire to better yourself.

You may be wondering where are we going with this. It is generally accepted that we have to obtain communication from the spirit world, but we never think that they may have a problem listening to us! All of these thoughts about how to control certain aspects through our mind are so that we can try and make our thoughts to the spirit world a more positive approach.

The next area in which the mind can be used is with the person to whom you are giving a message. If you send them thoughts to help them to understand the message, to be more open to what you are saying, then the whole communication should improve. It does not help to think why are spirit not giving me what I want, and also, what is the matter with this person who cannot accept the information that I am giving. Of course, you have to be sure that you are with the right person!

When working as a medium, in whatever way, we need to ensure that any misinformation that could be construed as our fault should be eliminated. Most mediums seem to think that our spirit friends can get over any obstacle that we might put in their way. My viewpoint is that we have always known that human beings have been fallible, so why should it be any different in this context? Any way that we can improve what we do, must be worthwhile. Therefore, it is important that we communicate properly with the spirit world. How often do we say to other people 'well you know what I mean' when our communication is unclear. Spirit may well have a problem with us in the same manner.

As with anything that we may do, we must be aware that there are boundaries over which we should not cross. To deliberately use our mind to influence anyone to do something, which is either illegal or dangerous, should never happen. Remember that we will have to atone for our wrongdoing either in this life or the next, so we cannot escape what will be. In my opinion, it is better for me not to cause any upset, injury or any other wrongdoing so that I do not have a problem later in this or the next life. Suffice to say, I am not, nor will I ever be, perfect. I just try for it.

CONNECTION WITH SPIRIT

Much has been said about spirit connection and one of the phrases is to 'sit in the power. When asked, many mediums cannot adequately describe what that means. I mused with spirit, and this is what they suggest: There are two parts to the application. The first is to set the conditions and the second is to make it happen.

Before I provide all the information, there is a strong point that needs to be made. Nothing is achieved unless wholehearted effort is used. This is not a 'quick fix', but a procedure that needs repetition to ensure quality. Too many 'so-called mediums' think mediumship is something that is easily picked up and put down. To succeed, there needs to be both application and perseverance. Because the subject is mental mediumship, there obviously needs to be some input mentally. Perseverance is absolutely necessary to achieve the best quality of mediumship.

THE CONDITIONS

Imaging sitting in a chair, and that you are surrounded by a large globe, with the top open. Allow yourself to feel comfortable in this situation. When you are ready, allow your thoughts to go out to your (main) guide. Invite your guide into your globe and ask that he/she brings a specific aroma, and to fill the globe with it.

Next, ask for your guide to allow you to feel their presence and the power that they bring with them and fill the globe. Take your time and allow the feelings that you have to build up. Over many of these sittings, changes will take place. You need to reach the point where your guide becomes strong within your aura, and over time the time taken to do this will take only a few moments.

The next stage is when, with your mind, you reduce the aroma and power in its projection to about six inches from your body. This will increase the power. When this is achieved, let the globe disappear, and adjust your senses to retain the power.

Once these levels have been achieved, become aware of your surroundings, but retain the power and aroma. After some practice, you should be able to carry on a conversation without losing the power. Nobody said that this was easy!

MAKING IT HAPPEN

There are many ways that have been taught on how to make spirit communication and how to select the person who is going to receive the massages. Many get a few pieces of information, say it out loud and hope for the best. It is too wishy-washy. The best demonstrations are when the medium knows who the recipient is and all the attendant information. Hoping for the best just does not work and only gives our critics more ammunition.

Every person in an audience, church or other venue will have people in the spirit world who want to communicate. It is not by chance that spirit has arranged the situation. I have unquestionable proof that once you start communicating, the correct spirit person WILL be there for the person who is the recipient.

Before connecting with a spirit person, who will give you information about a person at the venue, and before standing in front of your audience, link in with the spirit world. Ensure that you still have the power and the aroma close to you. Tell those who are waiting in the spirit world what you are going to do, and ask for their help in choosing the contact. Do not leave it to chance and hope for the best. Be professional.

To continue—select a person who will be your designated recipient. I use colours to make a contact. If someone has a bright colour on, I normally choose that person first. This is the person to whom you will give the spirit message. Having greeted the person, ask for their spirit friend/loved one to come close to you. The important bit here is that if you feel that you need to go to a particular person, then do it.

Explain to your recipient what your spirit contact looks like. Speak of their mannerisms. Next, give their relationship to the recipient. Lastly, pass on whatever message your spirit contact gives you. Do not give any more than that which you have been asked to do. You are a communicator for the spirit world. You are not their spokesperson. When you have completed your contact, thank both the spirit world communicator (mentally) and the recipient, then move on to the next communication. All the time, ensure that the power remains with you.

When all is completed, remember where you are with the (main) guide. Mentally, go back to your globe and thank all who have worked with you. Your guide will then retire and the aroma will dissipate. When all is back to the beginning allow the globe to disperse. If, along the way, you become uncertain or feel the contacts slipping away, ask for the original aroma to be provided again, and take comfort that your friends in the spirit world will not let you down—although you may let yourself down if you do not work properly.

CHAPTER 15

PHYSICAL WORK

The physical work that is being referred to here is not digging up a road! Physical work takes place in a séance room, and refers to the physical materialisation of spirit and also includes trance and transfiguration. The preparation to ensure that it conforms to a reasonable standard is sometimes a bit difficult. Therefore the following information on how to set up a séance room is given here.

Most séances are operated in complete darkness. The main reason is that ectoplasm can be burnt out with white light, which can cause physical damage to the medium. This does not preclude the thought that ectoplasm will never be seen in the light. There are situations that are currently developing, whereby spirit will bring their own light, but not white light. Sometimes, ectoplasm may withstand light in the red part of the spectrum, but this is not so in every case. Years ago, materialisation took place in white light, but the mediumship is not as strong now as it was then.

The preparation of a suitable room may take some time. I normally take half an hour to do this, but it was only after a trial and error period of making the room clean and light tight. Originally it took me up to 2 hours. The room must be cleaned very carefully, to ensure that the carpet is clean and that there is no dust anywhere. Ectoplasm is made up of bodily fluids, mainly from the medium, and returns from whence it came. Ectoplasm can pick up dirt that can then enter the medium's body. If there is a cabinet, then this area must also be checked for cleanliness. In our séance room, all our light bulbs are removed, together with any electrical apparatus that is not required. Electricity makes a difference to the energy levels, but there has been insufficient research to determine just how. As an aside, one of the spirit controls with one medium played with the controls on the tape player, turning the volume up and down. It was disconcerting to be suddenly blasted with full volume.

If there is a possibility to fabricate a room, then there is a further item that should be considered. Ventilation does not equate too well with a light tight room. To this end two boards are required, one for the inlet and one for the exit of air. Mounted on the two boards should be a system that incorporates at least seven right angles. The seven right angles will preclude light. The system could be made of black plastic guttering down pipes. Fine mesh could be placed over the outer ends. The two boards could then be located within the wall structure. On an exterior wall could be placed the 'exit air' system with an extractor fan, with a variable control on the inside wall. This situation will ensure adequate ventilation.

Each venue has different requirements for ventilation, and if a purpose built room is not possible, supplementary facilities need adding. A ceiling fan can be fitted and used with the agreement from spirit. There have been times when they have requested it be switched off, and then they hung a drum on one of the paddles. Care then needs to be observed. A portable air conditioning unit is another useful tool, although they can be noisy. This is also used in agreement with spirit, and they are very astute about its use, telling us when to switch on and off. In a limited seating area, a portable air conditioning unit will take up the space of one sitter. Each venue has different requirements for ventilation.

If there are windows, these need to be made light tight. The way that I use, is to fit a board that covers the outside of the window, with a piece of wood that acts as a prop, to ensure that it does not fall down. On the inside, I have fitted Velcro around the window, and the other part of the Velcro is glued to a piece of light tight material, similar to that which is used to make blinds. It then becomes fairly simple to connect the two pieces of Velcro and the room becomes completely dark. If there is an outside door, it may be necessary to fit thick curtains to preclude light. Usually, a black curtain is draped behind where the medium sits to allow for better definition during the séance.

All items that are not needed should be removed from the séance room. Chairs, to accommodate the sitters, should then be placed in a circle, to include the cabinet where the medium sits. The chairs should be of an upright type and consideration should be made as to whether flip-up seats (which take up less space) could be used balanced against seating large persons. If space is at a premium, a large person can take the space of two seats, so numbers must be considered. The cabinet, which is in our room, comprises two walls and two curtains. The curtain runners are fixed directly to the ceiling and hang to the floor. One curtain is fixed and the other is moveable. The moveable one is certainly used to its fullest extent, at high speed, by spirit.

The number of sitters may vary. There are instances where a large room can have many sitters, or sometimes just a few. I think that the energy levels really dictate the number of sitters. Previously there were up to 20 people in our room, arranged in two rows, but conditions were cramped. Our spirit friends then requested that we reduce the number of people and now we have a comfortable layout. Generally, the room size determines the number of people.

Having completed the light-tight aspect and the seating requirements, the next thing to consider is what else is required: a red light source that can be controlled by a dimmer switch, and a small table to stand the light on, a CD or tape player for the music that will be used and recording device for all the speech and sounds that will be heard. In the groups that I have had the privilege to attend, there is often a child from the spirit world, and they like to play with toys. Generally toys that can be included are: a toy drum (including drum sticks), a flute, a mouth organ and a small bell or two. One of our bells has a patch of luminosity attached so that it can be visible in the dark.

The light source consists of a box with one side open, painted matt black inside and out, and a light fitment inside. You may wish to experiment with different coloured light bulbs. We usually use red, but have on occasion used green and blue. The dimmer switch needs to be chosen carefully as they are normally rated against the wattage of the bulb. If you use a 40-watt bulb with a dimmer switch rated for 60-watts, the light will flicker. I have found that a sliding dimmer is better than a torroidal type as it is more consistent.

The music to be used is normally chosen by the medium. Whether a compilation on a CD or a tape is chosen, depends on the resources available. Generally, there needs to be lively music, but pop to classical is fine. The player needs to have simple controls, as most of the use will be in the dark, this means that someone needs to be well versed in its use. Often, the people in the circle are requested to sing, so there needs to be someone to organise this. Again, they need to be lively to bring up the energy level. If the player is a dual tape player, then two different sets of music can be used, such as the medium's choice and singers' choice.

As our memory is not perfect, a recording device is ideal for remembering everything that has happened. This is another area where choice of recorder can make a huge difference to what is recorded. I have a special microphone that I obtained from Germany, which picks up any sound in any part of the room. I use a minidisc recorder that can be set for up to 5 hours, which is more than ample time. Often there are sounds on the recording that were not heard during the time of the recording.

One further item that needs addressing is security. There are two doors in our room, one external and one internal (directly behind the medium). Both of these doors are fitted with locks. The external door is locked before we start, and the internal door is locked as soon as everyone (including the medium) is inside. It would be unfortunate for the medium's health if someone entered during a séance. Before anyone meets for the sitting, but after the room has been prepared, loud music is played to boost the energy level in the room. It is turned down or off just before the people congregate.

Before the people are seated, there needs to be a statement that nobody leaves until the séance is finished, and that then prompts the use of both the toilet and the consideration as to whether everyone is happy about sitting in the dark for a couple of hours or so. Each person should be provided with a glass (preferable plastic) of water and maybe a spare jug of water for sharing.

Before the doors are locked and the medium entering the room there needs to be a statement about what is going to happen. This is to do with both the security of the room and also the health of the medium. Each person needs to know why they are being locked in a room, possibly with other people that they do not know, what is required of them, and in the dark!

Different mediums have different requirements. For instance, one may allow the sitters a reasonable movement to drink water and to wipe their nose, so long as they do not get up and move around. Another may request that there is no movement whatsoever, without asking permission. Some mediums use a black cover for their heads, such as a balaclava folded up above the ears, and most wear black clothes. This is to allow the features to be more clearly seen. All jewellery is removed from the medium as it can leave burn marks during and after the séance. I have referred to the medium as being male, as that is the situation at home, regardless of who the medium is. This is in no way a chauvinistic attitude.

Returning to the security aspect, some mediums demand that each person sitting leaves all their personal possessions outside, and if that is so, separate plastic bags may be required for those articles. No lighters, no cameras, no mobile 'phones, no handbags (and to lighten the mood, I always include the males attending), no matches, no alarm watches, no luminous watches, nothing that could cause a problem. Additionally, a body search is sometimes requested. As this is, for me, going a bit too far, what we do is to only invite those people that we know, or can be vouched for by someone else.

It is sometimes useful to allow the sitters a couple of minutes in the dark before the actual séance begins. This should sort out those that are uncertain of sitting in the dark and those with a tendency to claustrophobia. If a person has a cold, they are not allowed in, as the cold together with the ectoplasm will cause real problems for everybody, especially the medium. As the energy (in our group) is supplied by the medium (50%), my wife and I (20% each), the rest comes from the other sitters, it becomes obvious that when the energy is translated into ectoplasm, we do mix things up, and a cold would not be nice.

Information should be given as to what will, or may, happen. The most important thing to tell people is that if they feel something touching them, they must not touch or grab where they feel movement. This is usually ectoplasm, which is mostly made from the mucus from the orifices of the medium. If this is touched without permission, the medium can suffer with great pain and lasting effects, such as bruising. In a worst case it can cause death of the medium.

On one occasion, in our room, one man felt something touching his shoes. He made a grab at it, but luckily did not touch it. It was ectoplasm. It returned into the medium's body so fast that it caused great pain. I immediately closed the circle, took the medium out and had someone care for him. The culprit, who was a friend, was banned forever. The medium suffered extensive bruising and was in pain for about a week. What had happened was one of the guides, who came through as a young lad, usually took great delight in tying the shoelaces of both shoes together, and that was what the man felt.

An area that may be a problem to a lay person is that, on occasion, the medium is moved about by spirit. That is to say, standing up, moving their arms and walking around. In the past there have been cries of 'fake', but those who do not understand how the trance situation works do this. All physical phenomena are controlled by energy, and spirit will use the energy in the most productive way. Having said that, there are some people who profess to be a trance medium and they are being totally deluded. For someone who has not got the experience, it may be difficult to distinguish between a competent trance medium and a fake, so common sense has to be used.

Each séance is different, but the leader should be able to give a very clear summary of what will ensue. This covers who will possibly come through and what to expect from each personality. The reason for this is to ensure that there is an awareness from each person so that nothing is missed. A dim light is usually on during the talk.

Once everyone is seated, sometimes the sitters are moved around to balance the energy. This is often done by using a pendulum, to differentiate between positive and less positive types of energies. It does not help if there are two or three people who have very strong energies sitting together, so that is why it is done. With everyone settled, the person in control (or leader) by the controls and the doors locked the session can begin.

Once the medium is seated, the leader will restrict the medium's movements by using either cable ties or Velcro. This should then be checked by at least two of the sitters to ensure that the medium is secured to his chair. All lights are turned off and the medium's choice of music is played. This is now the time that the medium 'goes into trance'. Trance levels are different for different mediums, but normally the medium is totally unaware of the proceedings in this situation.

Usually, the next thing that happens is that the main guide will request that the music is either turned off or reduced in sound level. The leader has to be very aware. Once the music has been turned off, the recorder is switched on. From this point on the variation can be quite surprising between different mediums.

Speech from spirit can come in a number of ways. The medium's voice box can be used; an external voice box can be built out of ectoplasm, just in front of the medium; or there can be a voice box created in a different part of the room. Although the voices are easily recognisable through the medium's voice box, the quality of sound is better through the external voice box. I remember one time when we were playing a song by Louis Armstrong. The music was right by the side of me, but he was singing at the same time from the opposite corner of the room (which everyone heard), and when the music stopped he just said 'Byee' from the same corner.

The following is a séance that my wife (Eve) and I (as leader) sat in which was held in June 2000, just to give an idea of what is possible.

The medium was David Thompson, who I consider to be the finest materialisation medium at this present time. By reading this that follows, you will understand how our relationship is with the spirit world and how a typical séance works.

Tim is a 'young' guide who is very cheeky.

Main Guide: Maybe you will ask the people to sing, to create the vibrations for our experiment tonight?

Eve: Shall we sing wartime songs?

All agreed. All singing.

Tim: Hello. Hello everyone.

All: Hello Tim. Welcome. How are you?

Tim: I'm alright, it's all the others.

Laughter

Tim: We are going to try a little experiment tonight. You have to listen carefully to what I'm going to say. It's got to be done in the proper way, so it doesn't hurt him in the chair (medium). You've got to follow everything to the letter. We are going to show you something. I'm going to do something about what 'the old boy' (me) has talked about before.

Laughter

Eve: (to me) Do you know what it is?

Me: Green light.

Tim: What light?

Me: Green.

Tim: No it ain't.

Me: Do I get another guess or not?

Tim: Just a little one.

Me: A different colour?

Tim: I'll thump him in a minute.

               Laughter There was a short discussion
                 as to whether he would or not.

Me: (panicking) No, Tim's good!

Tim: There's a reason that I'm a bit subdued. It's because
               I'm saving the energy.

Eve: OK. We understand.

Me: Whatever you want to do, it's up to you.

Tim: Put the music on please. I'll tell you what to do.

Me: How loud do you want the music?

Tim: Normal loud.

               Music on. Everyone either sings or hums.

Tim: Turn the music up.

               After a while.

Eve:	Turn it down. (Because I control the music, sometimes the instructions cannot be heard. Eve is on the other side of the cabinet and can hear more clearly).
Me:	Is someone talking?
Eve:	Yes.
Tim:	Turn the music off.

Music off.

Tim:	You've got to listen very, very carefully.
All:	Alright.
Tim:	Everybody stand up. 'Brommers' (me) you've got to be very careful as it is very dangerous for him in the chair (medium). Hold hands with the person in front of you (across the room).

This effectively covers all the room area.

Me:	Concentrate now. Is everyone holding hands?
All:	Yes.
Tim:	'Brommers', you and Evie-weevie (Eve) drop one of your hands close to the cabinet. Face the cabinet. Step forward, close to the cabinet.
Me:	Just the two, or all of us Tim?
Tim:	Just you 'Brommers'. Just in front of the cabinet.
Me:	Yes. (signifying that it had been done).

Tim:	Get your hand and touch the wall behind you. Evie-weevie, step close to the cabinet.
Eve:	Yes, I'm here.
Tim:	Open the curtain.

Curtain opened.

Tim:	Be very careful. Just touch the middle of the chair.
Eve:	How can I touch the middle?
Me:	Between his legs?
Eve:	He's not there! He's not there! He's gone (referring to the medium).
Guest:	Wonderful (excitedly).
Me:	Just keep it together.
Tim:	Step back. Close the curtain.

Curtain closed.

Tim:	Everybody sit down.
All:	Marvellous! Marvellous!
Tim:	Put the music on. Everybody sing and hum.

Music on.

Tim:	'Brommers, Brommers'. Turn the music off. Switch the (red) light on. (This has to be plugged into the wall, the wall switch switched on, then the dimmer

switch operated.) Check that he is in the chair and that the binds are on.

Eve: Good God! I can't believe that. That was marvellous Tim.

Light on.

Eve: I've moved the curtain. Good God!

Me: Would you two like to come and check? Yes, both of you. (This to two people who had witnessed the original binding and checked it, using cable ties.)

Eve: He had disappeared.

Me: Make sure that you check each side. You can touch him.

Brief gasps of amazement from all,
and agreement that it was amazing.

Eve: That really was something, wasn't it.

Me: Are you all sitting down?

Light off.

Me: Right Tim.

Tim: I'm back.

Me: So am I.

Eve: That was wonderful Tim. Absolutely wonderful.

Tim: Do you know why we got everybody to stand up and join hands?

Eve: Why is that then, love?

Tim:	So that you were aware that nobody could be in the room.
Eve:	Of course!
Me:	You're clever aren't you?
Tim:	Do you want to know how I did it?
All:	Yes.
Tim:	It's a trade secret.
Eve:	(laughing) Trade secret?
Tim:	We dematerialised him and levitated him up so that he was above the cabinet—above the ceiling.
Me:	Above the ceiling?
Tim:	Yeah. Well not actually, but up against the ceiling.
Eve:	That's a first. Well you can give yourself a big medal tonight.
Tim:	Whey hey! Have one for everybody.
Eve:	That was wonderful.
Guest:	There is something in front of us.
Tim:	It ain't me 'cause I'm talking to him in trance.
Guest:	He's pulling the curtain.
Tim:	It was more likely old Jack. (one of the spirit team)

Eve: Can I just say Tim, is the fan OK? (referring to the ceiling fan, which is on)

Tim: We had to keep him (medium) in the cabinet; he was screwed up, just like a little ball.

Eve: Is the fan too fast?

Tim: No, it's all right.

Me: Right, over to you, what do you want to do?

Tim: Put the music on. I'll see what else I can do. You might have lots of music tonight so that we can do lots of things.

Eve: Brilliant. That's absolutely brilliant.

                    Music on

Eve: (sensing) Somebody is standing in front of me.

Tim: Evie-weevie?

Eve: Yes, darling?

Tim: Turn the music down.

                    Music turned down.

Tim: Evie-weevie?

Eve: Yes, sweetheart?

Tim: Is that a new chair you're sitting on? (Tim broke the leg of a previous one) Do they cost a lot of money?

Eve: No, not that much. Why? What are you going to do?

Tim: I'm told that I'm not allowed to do anything.

Eve: Of course you are. You know you can do anything.

Tim: 'Brommers'

Me: What?

Tim: Are we allowed to do something to one of your chairs?

Me: So long as you don't break it.

Eve: He can't do it then.

Tim: I'll bend the chair.

Me: If you bend it, it will be a lot of money down the drain. You'll have to pay us back.

Tim: How much does it cost then?

Me: More than you can afford, mate.

Eve: He's moving the back of my chair (the chair back is against the wall).

One of the guests had the back of her chair pushed.

Tim: Don't worry missis, it won't hurt you.

Guest: I can't go forward.

Tim: Just relax.

Guest: I am relaxed.

Eve: Have you felt the chair, Tim?

Tim:	I'm just trying to do something, but you'll get annoyed.
Eve & me:	No, we won't get annoyed.
Eve:	If you bend it, you'll just have to bend it back again. That's the problem, because it's aluminium.
Me:	Once you've bent it, it won't go back.
Eve:	Oh, right. It's a bit difficult. Perhaps you could do somebody else's chair (being plastic).
Tim:	Heh heh.

General laughter.

Me:	He's got a wicked sense of humour, hasn't he?
Eve:	He's obviously thinking what he can do.
Tim:	I'll screw it up like a little ball.
Eve:	Oh no! Where am I going to sit if you do that?
Me:	That would be a good trick, to squeeze it up into a little ball and then straighten it out again. It would be really good.
Eve:	With me in it!

Laughter

Tim:	Maybe I'll dematerialise 'Brommers'.

Laughter

Me:	You can do what you like with me.

Eve (to Tim):   He loves you to bits and you can do what you like.

Tim: 'Brommers' turn the music up. All hold hands.

Music turned up.

Me: Hold hands until I tell you to let go (being aware of the need for constant energy).

Eve (shouting):   Oh! Oh! He's got my chair—it's not stopped him.

Me: They are taking a lot of energy.

Tim swings the curtain from side to side.

Me: (sensing a pull) No, you can't pull my trousers down! (Then, after more activity) No, take your hands out of my pocket! Is that you Louise?

Louise (spirit) tries to take my wedding ring. Timothy lifts the tape player and puts it on my lap. Timothy then has another try at pulling my trousers, but this was in time to the music.

Me: Oh thank you!(sarcastically)

Eve: What's the matter?

Me: There's water all over me.

Tim then proceeds to splash water over all and sundry accompanied by squeals and shrieks from the recipients. (We have water to drink, as sometimes it gets quite warm)
After a while, when only music is playing:

Eve: He's too quiet. There must be something going on.

Me: The quiet before the storm.

Guest: It's got very dark. Eve agrees. (There are different degrees of darkness when sitting in a blacked out room)

When the next track of music starts, knocking is heard outside of the room. (Nobody can gain access to any other part of the house or garden, as all security checks have been done)

Eve: It's above the ceiling! It's in the roof!

More knocking on the roof.

Eve: Well done Tim.

Tim then proceeds to use Eve's cooler (a fan and water-squirter combined) on everyone. He then transfers his attention to a football rattle, which he operates right in front of our faces. Then he plays with the drum in time to the music, mimicking the drummer on the piece of music. He eventually plays the drum with both sticks, blows a whistle and operates the rattle, all at the same time.

Tim: 'Brommers' turn the music off.

Music off.

Me: Can we let go of our hands now?

Tim: Yes. Let go everybody.

Drumming started for a short time.
This is quite different to that heard before.

Tim: We are going to let a new person come through.

Eve: Good.

Tim: You've got to listen to the drumming first of all.

Me: That's fine. Whatever you want to do.

Tim:	Just stick the music on. Just for a minute.

Music on.

Tim:	'Brommers', turn the music off.

Music off.
A spirit person enters the room and started drumming, using a different style.

Eve:	Brilliant, brilliant.
Me:	Somebody is standing out there, doing that. Welcome friend.
Spirit person:	My name is Zacharias.
Eve:	Hello. You are very welcome. You play the drums good.
Zacharias:	Zacharias.
Eve:	That's a nice name.
Zacharias:	I passed over in the war.
Me:	Which war was that?
Zacharias:	It was the battle of Marston Moor.

Small discussion as to when that was.

Guest:	The Boer war?
Me:	No. The civil war (in England).
Zacharias:	I was a parliamentarian.
Me:	You are most welcome.

Eve: It's lovely that you can come and visit us.

Me: Will you be coming again?

Zacharias: Could I just say, we defeated Prince Rupert on 2nd July 1644.

Eve: Were you a drummer boy?

More drumming, finishing with a drum roll.
Everybody applauded.

Tim: He's gone.

Eve: He must have played the drums in the army.

Tim: Yes, he was a drummer.

Eve: Tell him when you go back, that we really appreciated that.

Tim: He's still here.

Me: Can I ask you Tim . . . .

Tim: Course you can.

Me: There must have been a reason for his coming.

Tim: He's another part of the cog in the wheel.

Eve Tim. Can I ask you something?

Tim: Course you can, Malcolm.

Eve: Did you take the light bulb out in the back bedroom?

A bulb was removed from a cluster of three, and placed on the bed.

Tim:	No, It was Zacharias.
Eve:	Was it? Oh, that's brilliant.
Tim:	He's helping me with some of the physical things.
Eve:	How about when I was in the bathroom, and everything was thrown into the bath in front of me? Who was that?
Tim:	I don't know who that was. Lots of spirit people come in and use the physical energy from the circle, to be able to manifest things. There's always going to be some energy here.
Eve:	It's been really good here tonight.
Tim:	Does anyone want to ask any questions?
Me:	I think that we were a bit gob-smacked at the moment. Does anyone have a question for Tim?
Guest:	I don't quite know how to ask this.
Me:	Give it a try. Give your name first, and then ask your question.
Guest:	I'm Margaret. My husband has been very ill and I'd like to know when he will get well again.
Tim:	He's going to get a little better. Better than what he has been. Eventually we'll get the answer for him. At present nobody knows anything. The doctor said he would go and see him.
Me:	Tim, were you around last night?
Tim:	'Brommers' hold this a minute.

Me:	Thanks very much. It's the drum.
Guest:	Just what you wanted.
Me:	Trying to drum up business, I suppose. Am I changing what I'm doing on Friday night? It seems a bit more physical, than straight transfiguration. Is that right?
Tim:	Hey, 'Brommers'. I said to you that it would be a knock on effect, didn't I?
Me:	Yeah.
Tim:	Because you are sitting in a circle the closer you are to us, the more it stimulates your own latent energy.
Me:	Thank you very much. Next question please.
Guest:	My name is Angela.
Tim:	Hello Angela.
Angela:	Will my friends be moving? They desperately want to move.
Tim:	I'll ask the man who knows. Hold on a minute.

Spirit person,

Jack:	Good evening.
All:	Hello Jack.
Jack:	How you all doing?
Eve:	We're all right, how are you?
Jack:	I understand there is a personal question?

Me:	Yes, for Angela.
Jack:	Let me have a look. Yes, I believe they will sweetheart.
Angela:	Will they move to a bungalow?
Jack:	That I can't tell you, me darling, but I know they will move. I don't know how soon, but they will. Maybe shorter than they anticipate.
Me:	Any more questions?
Guest:	My name's Joan. Can you tell me, the bar back home, will we be selling it soon?
Jack:	Yes. It's destined for other things, your work.
Joan:	Will it be soon or a long time?
Jack:	It might take a few months, me darling, but don't worry.
Me:	Here's a leading question for you Jack. Have they got many spiritual people where they live?
Jack:	I believe there are more than you realise. Let me tell you something. Your spiritual work is only just beginning.
Guest:	I'm Margaret. I'm very interested in the spirit world and I believe in it. My girl friend who was with me last night, has to leave our group. Can you tell me why? It's not right for her. She has to leave.
Jack:	Yes, my darling. You have got to understand that everybody is not ready for this type of mediumship. Some people are, and some ain't. You've got to understand that we are all different. Some people feel

comfortable and others don't. Some people don't like the fact that they are sitting in darkness. You've got to understand that it is paramount for us to have this darkness for the safety of our medium. If she sat there and didn't feel comfortable, she may have unbalanced the whole energy.

Guest: I'm Dennis, as you probably know.

Jack: Yes. I know you.

Dennis: About 10 years ago, I wrote several screen plays for a film, and because nobody was buying, I put it to one side some time ago, but it seems to be rising to the surface again, and I don't know why that is. Does the spirit world have any thoughts on this?

Jack: Sometimes you have to get the message over, but in a subtle way. Maybe it's a bit of inspiration from our side for you to continue writing, so that we can inspire you and get the message across in a nice subtle way. You sit down my friend, and put pen to paper and see what happens.

Jack: 'Brommers' me old mate, do I sound any different?

Me: Yes, you do.

Jack: It's the ectoplasm. It's a little bit different tonight because of what we've had to do. It took a great deal of ectoplasm and it mucks up the machinery.

Me: That was Woweee, wasn't it (referring to the night's activities).

Jack: We are trying to do little bits and pieces.

Eve: Can I ask you a question?

Jack: Yes, of course you can sweetheart.

Eve: Not everybody agrees with others. When we go over to the spirit world, do you lose that? Or do you still have, not heated arguments, but argue?

Jack: Yes, of course you do. There are still uncertainties. You maybe approach it in a different way.

Eve: That's interesting. If everybody was really, really nicer, it would get a bit boring.

Jack: Do you know the biggest problem? It's to overcome those little idiosyncrasies you see in other people, and not allowing it to become something that affects you, and your own spiritual self.

This was the end of the tape. What subsequently transpired, was that some of our spirit friends came and said goodnight to us all.

I would recommend that anyone who is interested should look at David's website. If you get a chance of a sitting, then take it. He lives in Sydney, Australia and all the information can be found on www.silvercordcircle.com.au

Apart from the materialisation and trance, he is also an excellent mental medium.

CHAPTER 16

BALANCING

INTRODUCTION

The balancing to which I refer is for both the aura and chakras. In Chapter 17, I mention that my wife was ill after carrying out an exorcism. It was only through help of a knowledgeable medium friend that she got well. Her chakras were out of balance. Once they were corrected, she became her normal self, hence the need for an understanding of this subject. There are a number of ways of carrying out both types of balancing. What I give here is that which I am aware of, although there are other ways of balancing. Each balancing can be approached from two different perspectives; as an individual trying to balance oneself, or as a healer helping someone else.

There are other ways that can be used for balancing, such as using singing bowls, using crystals (including a crystal wand) and smudging with a sage wand.

CHAKRA BALANCING—PERSONAL

It may sound silly, or even obvious, but a shower under a powered water system can work very well. This is also useful (apart from cleanliness) to brighten up a feeling of being jaded or slightly under par.

Within the healing area is a treatment called colour therapy, where the body is bathed in different coloured lights, depending on the problem. This can also be recreated by using the mind. Elsewhere I have said that the mind is the most powerful natural resource that we have within ourselves. If we use our mind to help ourselves, then wonderful things can happen.

First of all, choose a comfortable chair in a room that is at a reasonable temperature for you. Start at the feet and ensure that all your muscles are relaxed. This is done by tensing and relaxing all the muscles that you can. Refer, if you like, to the relaxation exercise in Chapter 4. The next thing is to take a few slow, deep breaths, allowing the exhalation to also be slow.

Be aware that you feel good and that you have the ability to successfully complete this exercise. The most intense chakra is the base or Kundalini, which has a colour of red. Many people think that it has to be bright red, but there are many who cannot cope with such a bright colour, therefore, pick the shade of red that you feel comfortable with. Mentally, allow this colour to move around the base of the spine, being aware of any 'stickiness' or other impediments. Let the colour circulate until there is a feeling of being comfortable in that area. The idea is to ensure that each chakra is clean, working properly and balanced.

Allow the mind to now focus on the sacral chakra. Using the same technique, and the colour of orange (choosing your shade) let that colour circulate until the comfortable feeling is felt. Work through each of the other chakras in the same way, using the shade of colour that is right for you. The solar plexus is yellow, the heart is green, the throat is indigo, the brow (or third eye) is mauve and the crown, either silver or gold, depending on which you feel comfortable with.

You may feel that the chakras will tend to rotate. This is quite natural. Each chakra rotates in opposition to the one that is adjacent to it.

Having gone through all the chakras, then imagine a pure white light completely enveloping your body. Stay in this relaxed condition for a short while. It is best not to rush around directly after carrying out this procedure, otherwise the full benefit will be undone.

Aura Balancing—Personal

Within a basic healing class, it is quite usual to test where each person's aura is. Placing a hand from one person in close proximity to another person's hand does this. By moving one hand so that the distance between the two changes, there will be a point that can be 'felt' where the two auras meet. For those who are not very spiritually aware, the distance is fairly small, maybe six inches. For those who have developed, the distance can be much more. Rubbing the hands together makes them more sensitive.

Starting at the top of the head, allow the hands to cup around it, but not on it. Let your thoughts lead you as to how to progress. If this is difficult, then imagine smoothing your aura from the top downwards, covering as much area as is possible. For the areas that you cannot cover, let your mind take you over those areas, leaving your hands just away from the body, near the heart. It will take a little time to get into this way of balancing, but it will come.

Chakra Balancing—Assisted

The person who is being balanced needs to sit on an upright chair in the Egyptian meditation position. All the limbs and body should be brought to a relaxed state by tensing and relaxing as many muscles as possible. The person carrying out the balancing should have good knowledge of chakras and how they work. Additionally, they should be a sensitive or a medium as visualisation of the chakras is required. Often it is best to have some relaxing type music playing in the background. I find that if I put my hands just above the top of the person's head to be balanced, there is some positive change in their relaxation.

From there, each chakra needs to be either looked at or sensed to see what (if any) problem there is. The mind of the balancer controls all that happens. By using the hands energy can be provided where required. I suggest using a gentler colour that is associated with each chakra to thoroughly cleanse all around the area.

Working through each chakra in turn, using the appropriate colours, ensure that each area is left in the best possible state. When this part has been completed, ask the person being balanced how they feel. If there is still a feeling of imbalance, then a second balancing should be carried out. When all is completed, and the person being balanced is satisfied, use the mind to completely cover the person with a white light with a thought of sealing all the stable feelings within that person.

A word of caution then needs to be given to the person being balanced, and that is, they should not do anything to bring the unwanted situation back. It may seem a silly thing to do, but the changed situation may cause an initial feeling of being 'off balance' to that person, and they may think that they do not feel 'right'. Any change that occurs in our body will eventually become the norm, but that does not mean that it is right. When the body is brought back to what it should be it would take a little time for that to become the norm.

I always feel that a small prayer would round off the treatment.

AURA BALANCING—ASSISTED

Repeat the first paragraph under Chakra Balancing—assisted

The balancer should detect where the aura is and work from that position. First of all, commencing with the head, stroke the aura in a downward motion, using the mind to ensure that any areas that are muddy or brown have more attention. Continue, following the body contours, but also remembering that no touching is required.

Using the thought that brighter colours reflect a better disposition of the person, try and improve the general sense of the aura. Again, changes may initially confuse the person, but after a short period of rest, everything should be back to normality.

CHAPTER 17

EXORCISM

WARNING!

This is not information that can be used by people who are just beginning work with spirit. The information contained here should only be used by competent mediums who understand their own, and the people associated with them, complete protection.

Exorcisms should not be attempted by anyone who is either uncertain of their spiritual beliefs or is unwell. Additionally, it should be noted that this can be dangerous.

At the end of this chapter I have added information as to how you can protect yourself against a psychic attack.

Before contemplating an exorcism, due regard MUST be made to whether or not it is relevant. There are three main areas where initial thought may be that one is required, but careful consideration and the use of common sense needs to be addressed. The three areas are: mental instability or a behavioural problem, non-malicious spirit contact and malicious spirit contact. The first needs to be pointed towards a doctor. The second can usually be sorted out by a good medium, as there are times when the spirits can be left alone and the concern can be explained. This chapter is concerned with the third area.

Exorcisms are normally carried out by someone who is entirely competent. It is not for the enthusiastic amateur! The important point to remember is not to move outside the area of expertise. Too many things can happen, that, if not prepared for, will cause more problems than were there previously. This aspect cannot be stressed too much! For those who do not believe me, I must stress that to carry out an exorcism without understanding what they are doing are, in effect, opening themselves up to influences that they will not be able to control. This could lead to illness, mental illness or death. YOU HAVE BEEN WARNED!

There have been various recent cases of exorcism where the death of the person subjected to the exorcism has followed. The person carrying out the exorcism has been convicted of their death.

There is a difference in approach to each faith, and to those who may use the power of exorcism. Generally, only priests of the Roman Catholic faith, who have been trained, may carry out the Catholic exorcism, although there is a simple exorcism that may be used by the laity. Other Christian exorcisms may be carried out by the laity. Also included is an exorcism that I have used myself. The Jewish religion treats a 'possession' with healing and is carried out by a Rabbi and nine others, using a rams horn trumpet. Hindus use the holy book (veda) Adharva for casting out demons. Islamic clergy carry out exorcisms. As far as I know, the only group that does not subscribe to exorcisms is the Sikh religion.

As this is a subject that is not normally come across by average people, care must be taken. First of all one has to be sure that an exorcism is appropriate. There are many situations where the being (spirit, ghost, etcetera) is benign, beings that just inhabit a space and do not mean any harm to us. They may give a few frights to people who are unused to such beings, but if they cause no harm, I either leave them be or ask them to go, depending on the circumstances.

The circumstances must be established before any 'gung ho' action happens. A person who is sensitive to spirit (a good medium) is of great help. The being could be a family member. At one requested 'supposed' exorcism, it transpired that an aunt (in spirit) had appeared to a teenager showing pictures of animals. The teenager was very emotional and scared. When the aunt was asked why she was doing this, she said that she was showing her nephew views of his future and that he would be going to Africa later in life.

It was suggested that it was not a good idea to frighten the lad, and was asked to desist until he was older and had come to terms with the place called the spirit world. This she agreed to do. Therefore this was not an acceptable exorcism, but a talk with someone in spirit who was not aware of a problem until it was pointed out. We have to be aware that our relatives in spirit often wish to help us, but if we are unaware of their presence it can be a bit of a shock.

There is a very great need for a complete understanding of the parameters for an exorcism. There is also a great need for understanding how spirit work. I fully endorse the attitude of using mental mediumship to establish the ground rules before ANY work is started. I am also highly concerned that anyone without sufficient appreciation of what goes on, jumping in and saying that they can carry out an exorcism. This is not for the layperson. Any person carrying out an exorcism MUST have had real experience of working with spirit, understand what the reality is of working with spirits that can really be nasty, and also be a stable and fit person.

Before moving to the actual exorcism, it should be noted that there are differing beliefs, and the one that I have provided is essentially for Christians. Different religions have different beliefs, and therefore dealing with evil forces may not be undertaken in quite the same way. It would be offensive to carry out a Christian exorcism in the confines of people with a differing belief.

The Vatican has published a new 'rite' for exorcism, but these have been expressly put together for the use of suitably selected priests. It seems to be overlong from a layman's point of view, because it names all the saints, asks for delivery from various problems and requests protection for the possessed. A number of biblical texts are also invoked.

The Jewish Talmud contains references to exorcism, and other religions that have forms of ritual for exorcism are Hindu, Buddhist, Islamic and Shinto, and also Shamans of various tribal beliefs. Now that the 'West' has taken to *Feng Shui*, there seems to be similar rituals, using bells and singing bowls to get rid of 'negative energy'.

Sometimes there are influences that really ought to be got rid of. Again, one has to establish the situation properly. Just jumping in and carrying out an exorcism is not acceptable. Once the situation has been properly assessed, then one may proceed. Generally, there are two types of exorcism: a place and a person. These are the rituals that I use. I have to say that they have served me well so far, but there may be occasions in the future when I might change what I do, based on more experience. I am an ordained minister.

THE EXORCISM THAT I HAVE USED

EXORCISM OF A PLACE

The assumption is that the place is a house, and that an ordained minister is carrying out the exorcism.

Paraphernalia required: salt (in a suitable container), water (in a suitable container), an oval container (for the salt and water), incense and my clerical collar and stole.

Preparation

Minister, fully enrobed. Place the right hand over the container of salt, say these words:

I exorcise thee, creature of salt by the Living God, by the Holy God, by the Omnipotent God, that Thou mayest be purified from all evil influence, in the name of Him who is Lord of Angels and of men, Who filleth the whole earth with His Majesty and Glory. Amen.

We pray Thee O God, in Thy boundless Loving Kindness to stretch forth the Right Hand of Thy Power upon this creature of salt, which we bless and hallow in Thy Holy Name. Grant that this salt may make for health of mind and body to all who partake thereof and that there may be banished from the place where it is used, every power of adversity and every illusion or artifice of evil, through Jesus Christ Our Lord. Amen.

Place the right hand over the container of water, say these words:

I exorcise thee, creature of water by the Living God, by the Holy God, by the Omnipotent God, that Thou mayest be purified from all evil influence, in the name of Him who is Lord of Angels and of men, Who filleth the whole earth with His Majesty and Glory. Amen.

O God, who for the helping and safeguarding of men dost hallow the water set apart for the service of Thy Holy Church, send forth Thy Light and Power upon this element of water which we hallow and bless in Thy Holy Name. Grant that whoever uses this element of water in faithfulness of spirit, may be strengthened in all goodness and that everything sprinkled with it may be made holy and pure and guarded from all assaults of evil, through Christ Our Lord. Amen.

Put some water into the oval container, then cast the salt into the water three times in the form of a cross, using these words:

Let the salt and water mingle together in the Name of the Father and the Son and the Holy Ghost. Amen

O God, the giver of invincible strength and King of irresistible power, whose splendour shines through the whole of creation, we pray Thee to look upon this Thy creature of salt and water and to pour down upon it the radiance of Thy Love and Blessing and to hallow it, that wheresoever it may be sprinkled and Thy Holy Name invoked in prayer, there shall only reign love and peace and every noble aspiration be strengthened, every good resolve made firm and the fellowship of the Holy Spirit vouchsafed to us who place our trust in Thee. Thou Who with the Son livist and reignest in unity of the same Holy Spirit, God throughout ages. Amen.

Exorcism:

Commencing outside of the house, say:

Peace be to this house and all who dwell herein. In the Name of the Father and of the Son and of the Holy Ghost. Amen. May the Lord purify me that I may worthily perform this service.

Carrying a stick of lit incense (if required, a lit incense stick may be left in each room, ensuring that it is safe to do so), draw a line with the salt water across each entrance of each doorway, room, staircase or cupboard (salt water can also be sprinkled in corners and across beds and any other place that seems necessary), using these words:

We pray Thee O Lord so to bless this room/cupboard/staircase/etc. by Thy mighty Power that those who enter here leave behind all unworthy thought and feeling and that Thy children who dwell in this place may ever serve Thee in peace and holiness in life. Through Christ Our Lord. Amen.

After every room has been exorcised and before leaving the house, say this prayer:

O God Who in Thy Providence hast appointed a wondrous ministry of Angels, we pray Thee to send down Thy Holy Angel to bless and to hallow this house that they who dwell herein may live in the power and love of Christ Our Lord and Master and may continually serve before Thee in all good works through the same Jesus Christ Our Lord. Amen.

EXORCISM OF A PERSON

The assumption is that an ordained minister who is fully enrobed is carrying out the exorcism.

Paraphernalia required: salt, water, a container (for the salt and water) Incense and my clerical collar and stole.

Preparation

Follow the same routine as for preparation for exorcising a place.

Exorcism:

> Note: This may be more convenient if the person to be exorcised is sitting down on a dining room style chair.

Start with a prayer, saying these words:

Almighty God, the protector of all who trust in Thee, send forth Thy Power to keep us at this time both outwardly in our bodies and inwardly in ourselves that so far as it is expedient for us we may be defended from all adversities which may happen to the body and from all evil which may assault and hurt the soul, through Jesus Our Lord. Amen.

Then, making the sign of the cross, say these words:

In the Name of the Father and of the Son and of the Holy Ghost. Amen. May the Lord purify me that I may worthily perform this service.

Sprinkling salt water over the head of the person concerned, say these words:

In the Name of the Father, Jesus Christ the Son and the Holy Ghost in this power and by this authority I bid and demand all such evil influences to come forth from this person. Sprinkle salt water over the person. *I exorcise all such evil influences and seeds of evil.* Lay hands on the head of the person. *I lay upon them now the spell and power of Christ's Holy Church that they trouble not this servant of God.*

In God's Holy name, in the power of Jesus Christ, I call upon the Angel Hosts of Heaven to be about each one of us here that no evil influence may assault our bodies or souls and they take such influences to the realms of light. Amen.

One may think that that is the end of it, but unfortunately this is not always the case. One lady, who was exorcised, reacted in quite a different way. The way of exorcism became very loud, where the entity and the exorciser had a huge argument (the entity using the lady's voice). Because she had become so used to being possessed, she felt unbalanced and invited the entity to return. Just getting rid of evil does not mean that it will stay away, especially if invited back. The rest of this job entailed counselling, to ensure the lady's mind was kept positive.

I mentioned that it is not a good idea to carry out exorcisms without training, and to prove a point; the story behind the above exorcism is this. It was carried out by my wife, and eventually the entity said that they would leave if they could go through my wife's aura. Being somewhat inexperienced at that time, she agreed. She said that it was like an electric shock going through her, but that was not the end of it. For about three months she was quite ill. What had happened was that her whole system was out of balance, and it took another experienced medium some time to rebalance her. So—be warned

THE CATHOLIC EXORCISM THAT MAY BE USED BY THE LAITY

In the name of the Father, and of the Son, and of the Holy Ghost. Amen.

Most glorious Prince of the Heavenly Armies, Saint Michael the Archangel, defend us in our battle against the principalities and powers, against the rulers of this world of darkness, against the spirits of wickedness in the high places. Come to the assistance of men whom God has created to His likeness and whom He has redeemed at a great price from the tyranny of the Devil. Holy Church venerates thee as her guardian and protector; to thee, the Lord has entrusted the souls of the redeemed to be led into heaven. Pray therefore the God of Peace to crush Satan beneath our feet, that he may no longer retain men captive and do no injury to the Church. Offer our prayers to the Most High, that without delay they may draw His mercy down upon us, take hold of the dragon, the old serpent, which is the Devil and Satan, bind him and cast him into the bottomless pit that he may no longer seduce the nations.

In the name of Jesus Christ, our God and Lord, strengthened by the intercession of the Immaculate Virgin Mary, Mother of God, of Blessed Michael the Archangel, of the Blessed Apostles Peter and Paul and all the Saints, we confidently undertake to repulse the attacks and deceits of the Devil.

God arises; His enemies are scattered and those who hate Him flee before Him. As smoke is driven away, so are they driven; as wax melts before the fire, so the wicked perish at the presence of God.

Where an asterisk (*) is shown, the sign of the cross shall be used by the lay person.

We drive you from us, whoever you may be, unclean spirits, all satanic powers, all infernal invaders, all wicked legions, assemblies and sects. In the Name and by the power of Our Lord Jesus Christ, * may you be snatched away and driven from the Church of God and from the souls made to the image and likeness of God and redeemed by the Precious Blood of the Divine Lamb. *

Most cunning serpent, you shall no more dare to deceive the human race, persecute the Church, torment God's elect and sift them as wheat. * The Most High God commands you, * He with whom in your great insolence, you still claim to be equal. God who wants all men to be saved and to come to the knowledge of the truth. God the Father commands you. * God the Son commands you. * God the Holy Ghost commands you. * Christ, God's Word made flesh, commands you. * He who to save our race outdone through your envy, humbled Himself, becoming obedient even unto death, He who has built His Church on the firm rock and declared that the gates of hell shall not prevail against Her, because He will dwell with Her all days even to the end of the world. The sacred Sign of the Cross commands you, * as does also the power of the mysteries of the Christian Faith. * The glorious Mother of God, the Virgin Mary, commands you, * She who by her humility and from the first moment of Her Immaculate Conception crushed your proud head. The faith of the Holy Apostles Peter and Paul, and of the other Apostles commands you. * The blood of the Martyrs and the pious intercession of all the Saints command you. *

Thus, cursed dragon, and you, diabolical legions, we adjure you by the living God, * by the true God, * by the Holy God, * by the God who so loved the world that He gave up his only Son, that every soul believing in Him might not perish but have life everlasting, stop deceiving human creatures and pouring out to them the poison of eternal damnation; stop harming the Church and hindering her liberty. Begone, Satan, inventor and master of all deceit, enemy of man's salvation. Give place to Christ in Whom you have found none of your works; give place to the One, Holy, Catholic, and Apostolic Church acquired by Christ at the price of His blood. Stoop beneath the all-powerful Hand of God; tremble and flee when we invoke the Holy and terrible Name of Jesus, this Name which causes hell to tremble, this Name to which the Virtues, Powers and Dominations of heaven are humbly submissive, this Name which the Cherabim and Seraphim praise unceasingly repeating: Holy, Holy, Holy is the Lord, the God of Hosts.

God of heaven, God of earth, God of Angels, God of Archangels, God of Patriarchs, God of Prophets, God of Apostles, God of Martyrs, God of Confessors, God of Virgins, God who has power to give life after death and rest after work; because there is no other God than Thee and there can be no other, for Thou art the Creator of all things, visible and invisible, of Whose reign there shall be no end, we humbly prostrate ourselves before Thy glorious Majesty and we beseech Thee to deliver us by Thy power from all tyranny of the infernal spirits, from their snares, their lies and their furious wickedness. Deign, O Lord, to grant us Thy powerful protection and to keep us safe and sound. We beseech Thee through Jesus Christ Our Lord.

Amen

Holy water is sprinkled in the place where we are.

Psychic Attack

Psychic attacks do not normally happen to average people. There is usually a very good reason for it to happen, and one of the reasons is jealousy. There are other reasons such as hatred, annoyance and just plain nastiness. The instigator is usually either themselves, or is using someone, who is very powerful psychically. If anyone goes along the pathway of misusing psychic abilities, then they may well have taken on more than they will ever be able to cope with.

One of the worst psychic attacks that my wife and I had, lasted for just over a week. Every night we were subjected to real disturbances, we used the passive protection as shown below, and the reason that we used this was that if we were to be aggressive ourselves, we could cause more problems than we could cope with.

Protection From Psychic Attack

Although the physical and mental reactions to a psychic attack are pretty horrendous, the following procedure has sustained both my wife and myself in the past. We used the procedure for about a week, but the length of time is determined by experience. If the problem is still obvious, then carry on. If it lasts longer than about a week, then extra help may be needed.

Night time is when we are most vulnerable, and when in bed ready to sleep, imagine that you are surrounded by a mirror, which is entirely seamless, and with the reflecting side pointing away from you. A good concept is a vacuum flask. There should be no cracks or seams. If there are two of you, then imagine both of you entirely surrounded. The use of imagination works in a very positive way if you want it to. The mind is the most powerful tool that us humans have, although the majority of us are either not aware or 'pooh, pooh' the idea. Trust me, it is really powerful.

CHAPTER 18

LECTURING AND WORKSHOPS

SECTION 1 INTRODUCTION

Teaching is a very fulfilling task, whether it is by lecturing or running a workshop. Caution though, is required. If it is you who is teaching, then you need to be sure of your motives and more importantly, your abilities. If you are attending a lecture or workshop, then the cost must be matched against the learning. This is sometimes difficult, but the basic attitude should be; is the person in charge recommended. Unfortunately, I know of well-known mediums that are good at demonstrations, but can't teach at all. Here again, money is the objective, but there is also the possibility it could be ego.

WORKSHOPS—GENERAL

You as the student
The basic parameters that you need to know before you book a course are:

Who is teaching what, (are they qualified and have they got a good track record for what they are teaching)?

How many are there in each class (more than 15 becomes unwieldy and loses the personal touch)?

Who is your teacher and what sort of class are _you_ in?

Are the people in your class at the same level as you?

To what depth is it being taught (that is, is it for beginners, intermediate or advanced level)?

What facilities are provided (if it is more than one day; what are the sleeping arrangements and are they of a sufficiently reasonable standard; are there en-suite facilities or are they shared. What meals and other catering arrangements are there, including coffee/tea breaks)?

If you are a foreign student, what are the arrangements for a translator?

Are there sufficient breaks during the day (and if there is evening work, what is planned)?

Is the venue at a reasonable (cost and time) distance?

Essentially, is the product that is offered for purchase exactly what you want?

You as the organiser/teacher
Be absolutely clear as to what is being offered (and ensure that the teachers are not only able to demonstrate what they are teaching, but also that they have the ability to teach the chosen subject properly).

Get the finances right (calculate how much the venue will be, how much each teacher will receive, how much the catering costs, how much any incidentals, such as advertising, will cost, etcetera).
Then, decide the level of payment required from each student.

Ensure that the venue is booked and deposit paid (check at regular intervals that the booking is still viable).

Ensure that the teachers are booked (taking a chance on a teacher that is not experienced could lead to further workshops being poorly supported. Check at regular intervals that the booking is still viable).

Ensure that the teachers have any handouts or facilities available (including paper and pencils for the students, clipboards if necessary, and any other materials).

Ensure that the event is properly advertised in the correct papers (clarity is important for both the reader and printer. Remember to include a telephone number! Give sufficient detail, with detailed follow-up brochures to be sent by post).

If teaching abroad, then ensure that sufficient translators are available who can do the job properly (much time can be wasted through inadequate translations)

Also, if teaching abroad, ensure that the venue and other facilities are really up to standard and that they are sufficient for your needs.

One of the biggest problems with teaching, especially within the UK, is keeping the interest alive. I have found that in Europe there is such a thirst for knowledge, a slight lack of preparedness does not seem to be so much a problem.

Clear information over short periods is more easily digestible that a long day on one aspect of a subject. It is the same as any other teaching, and I am sure that there are many publications that can lead someone to improving their skills. I believe that each day that we live in this world, we learn more. This gives us the ability to fine-tune what we believe and also how to provide some of the wisdom to others that we each have stored for future reference.

Lecturing

This always seems easy, but the lecturer, more often than not, has agonised for a long time over getting everything right. It is not easy, but with diligence it can be quite productive.

Pre-production is the key. Whether one uses prompt cards or a fully printed out script, attention to detail is paramount. There needs to be humour—but it should go with what is being said, and not be out of context. When talking about a subject there needs to be 'light and shade' so as not lose the audience through boredom. The biggest asset is to thoroughly know the subject, because as with any talk, there will be questions afterwards!

Workshops and lectures are the means of transferring knowledge from one person to many others. If they are given in the right atmosphere and surroundings, then they are very good, but once silly little things go wrong it can become very difficult. Such things that we take for granted are heat and light. Just one of these can curtail any learning. Any preparation should cover as much as possible, with fall-back arrangements also in place.

Any class will have differing levels of understanding and abilities. To accommodate all who are in a class requires a certain amount of flexibility in the teaching process. I have always maintained that when teaching, the person who actually does the teaching should know far more than that which is in the curriculum. In that way there should be only a limited number of problems.

Last of all, I have a theory that if there are any problems, it is not the fault of the student; it is the fault of the tutor. If they do not learn what I teach, then it is my fault, and I have to reconsider as to what I should change as regards my teaching methods—including—am I the right person to do the teaching.

Now, to get down to the basics with lecturing, here are a few hints on how to present both yourself and your information:

If you are scruffy, people will not provide you with the attention that you may require! Therefore your total presentation has as much to say about your visual presentation as your script. Both need to be pristine. This will provide you with more confidence than that which you started. Speak in measured tones with light and shade, and speak clearly. Muttered words do not convey to the back of the room.

You must know your subject. If you are uncertain, then that will show and everyone will know that you are 'winging it'. The audience is expecting to hear something that they can take an interest in. Please do not disappoint them.

Remember that when you are going to speak more than you normally do, plus you are in the spotlight, you will probably have a dry mouth. It is worth while either having a good drink (of water) before you start or take sips (of water)—from a glass—as you progress. It has now become acceptable—some would say imperative—that a bottle of water is constantly with us. What goes in must come out, so also make sure that you have been to the toilet before you start.

If you are using visual aids, then that aid must be in pristine working condition. If using a blackboard, it needs to be very clean before you start—and that means before anyone else sees it. Be careful when using projectors. There is usually a tendency to completely darken the room. This gives the students the opportunity to doze off, so mornings are better than afternoons. Personally, I do not see the need to completely darken a room, but just to reduce any glaring light. Try things out before using them, especially in a similar situation, before the actual event.

If using somebody else's equipment at an unfamiliar location, then be there early to have a run through before the equipment is used in earnest. There is nothing worse than sitting through a lecture when the lecturer doesn't know how to use the equipment correctly, and then asking somebody in the middle of the lecture, for help.

Remember that in giving a lecture, the object of the exercise is to impart information to people who, maybe, are finding it hard to comprehend. This means that the tempo, loudness and enunciation are paramount, also the amount of information being given in each sentence. You may even have to repeat some pieces of information. The best way is not to repeat the same words over and over, but to give the information in a different way. The idea being that some people will understand straight away and others can understand more easily when the information is presented in a different way.

As you are giving information to the students, remember that you are not giving it to your notes, this means that you actually have to look at the people to whom you are speaking. This gives them the feeling that you not only, do know what you are talking about, but keeps them aware of what is going on, as they will feel guilty if you are looking at them and they are not paying attention. A smile and a humorous aside will also help, especially if it shows you in a more human light.

A page of text in Times Roman, 14 point will take about 3 minutes to read at a measured pace. So a 30-minute lecture needs only 8 to 10 pages, depending on the content. Each piece of information should take the student on to the next piece. If a student poses a question, then the next piece of information that you will be giving should answer the question. It should be in a logical progression. There are times when a synopsis of the lecture should be given either in an advertisement or prior to the actual lecture, so that your audience will understand what it is that you will speak about, and to what depth.

Never use long words when short—and more common—words can be used. Often, long words can lead to a misunderstanding when the student does not really understand what the long word meant. Additionally, while they are trying to work out what has just been said, they lose the next piece of information as well. One word of warning. Do not use another person's notes. They, more often than not, will not suit your personality or delivery. If you have to use basic material from elsewhere, then rewrite it to suit you.

When giving a talk or lecture, I go through my notes and put in extra punctuation marks. This shows me where I need to change the pace or delivery of that piece of information. In strictly grammatical terms it looks like rubbish, but it works for me. There are also times when I change to italics instead of quotation marks, just to give me a sense of the change that I need to impart. The end product must be to provide information to those who want to listen in an acceptable way.

The amount of people may make a difference to your feelings and emotions, but remember that people are just that, people. If you can deliver a lecture to one person, all that you are doing is adding a number. You may have to use a microphone or speak louder, but the principle remains the same—to impart information.

Your first words should project something about you. Should you be formal or informal? Would a 'Hi' be correct, or a 'Good morning'? It is too late to find out whether the microphone is switched on or not. Your first words will identify you. If you are precise in your welcome, students will expect you to be precise in the rest of the things that you say. Make sure that you get it right. If you have handouts, when will you give them out? If there is too much information in the handout, then what is the point of the lecture? Usually handouts are provided at the end of a lecture, as the recipients will automatically start reading as soon as they are in their hands.

Watch others to see their good and bad ways of delivering information. Obviously ditch the bad ones, but adhere to the good ones. If they work for one person, then they should work for you. Last of all practice what you are going to do. When I first started, I agonised over what I was going to say, and by using repetition, I can now (nearly) give a lecture with only a minimal preparation.

WORKSHOPS—SPECIFIC

To define what a workshop is, seems the best place to start. It is in a place where like-minded people get together to learn something in a practical manner. It may be to do with the hands or mind, but the principle is the same, to try and do what is being taught.

Preparation is very important. Each individual will progress at a different speed to the others; therefore the curriculum must take into account all individuals. Each person must be treated in exactly the same way as the others. There must be no favouritism. The workshop must include everyone who is taking part. It is bad planning if the day is over and there are still a couple of people who have not experienced the same as the others. Do not try to do too much.

Each workshop would normally be broken down into sessions. Each session could be about two hours in length because individuals require either a toilet or tea break. A suggested breakdown could be:

9am-10:45 1st session
11am-1pm 2nd session
1pm-1:45 Lunch
1:45-3pm 3rd session
3:15-5pm 4th session

If evenings are used (which I do when teaching abroad):

7pm-9pm 5th session

Other considerations are whether to provide teas/coffees and lunch (and dinner when applicable), or to ask the people to bring their own packed lunch and refreshments.

One of the biggest problems that can (and does) happen is when the person taking the workshop has a sudden attack of ego. Although it may be fascinating, hearing about what that person has done with their life, the real reason for the workshop is to impart information that can be absorbed and then used by the individuals who are attending the workshop. A small aside about one's personal life may be interesting to refocus people on what you are saying, but it should not be overlong.

It is not my intent to break down all possible scenarios, as there are so many possibilities. Planning is the key. Each of us provides information in different ways, which makes a difference to the approach and to the time allocated for each part of each subject. Sometimes each action that the student undertakes can take longer with one person than another, and that also has to be planned for.

CHAPTER 19

CHURCHES, CENTRES AND BELIEFS

Modern Spiritualism is commonly known to have started in 1848, with the Fox sisters obtained rappings from a person in spirit. This is so well documented, that I need not expand further. In 1951, the repeal of the Witchcraft and Vagrancy Act (in England) ended the unfair bias against mediums and allowed meetings to be open to the public rather than behind closed doors. The outcome allowed spiritualist churches and centres to open throughout the UK and the trend has gone to other countries, notably the United States, Canada and Australia.

Mediumship and healing are mentioned in the Bible a number of times, so they are nothing new. There have also been reports of direct voice and materialisation. All these things predate the Bible, so the abilities have always been there. The Oracle of Delphi and other oracles were actually mediums that had their own temples in olden times. In researching history, temples were based on the medium, who gave information to the servants of the temple, who in turn gave it to the general public. At some point, the servants of the temple decided to provide their own information based on political pressures of the day and do away with the mediums. We are aware that churches today, follow the doctrines of the order to which they belong, but when one starts to think about what has gone on previously, we are coming back to the original understanding that a medium gives messages from spirit. This is what happens in spiritualist churches and centres now.

In general there are three groups of spiritualists: those that believe there should be some form of Christianity within their belief, those that deny any sort of Christianity within their belief, and those who are open minded, but essentially believe that we are spiritual beings living in an earthly life. Within each group there are other groups that feel their organisation is run for the members who more closely adhere to their precepts.

The group that believes in an amalgam of Christianity and Spiritualism is under the banner of the Greater World Association Trust, often referred to as the Greater World or Christian Spiritualist. They are administered from 3 Lansdowne Road, Holland Park, London W11 3AL, England.

Its declaration of belief and pledge are:

1. I believe in One God Who is Love.
2. I accept the Leadership of Jesus Christ.
3. I believe that God manifests through the Illimitable Power of the Holy Spirit.
4. I believe in the survival of the human soul and its individuality after physical death.
5. I believe in the Communion of God, with His angelic ministers, and with the souls functioning in conditions other than earth life.
6. I believe that all forms of life created by God intermingle, are interdependent and evolve until perfection is attained.
7. I believe in the perfect justice of the Divine Laws governing all life.
8. I believe that sins committed can only be rectified by the sinner himself or herself, through the redemptive power of Jesus Christ, by repentance and service to others.
9. I will at all times endeavour to be guided by my thoughts, words and deeds by the teaching and example of Jesus Christ.

The other group, which rejects any association with Christianity, is under the banner of the Spiritualist National Union, often referred to as the SNU. Their beliefs are based on seven principles. These are:

1. The fatherhood of God.
2. The brotherhood of man.
3. The communion of spirits and the ministry of angels.
4. The continuous existence of the human soul.
5. Personal responsibility.
6. Compensation and retribution hereafter for all the good and evil deeds done on earth.
7. Eternal progress open to every human soul.

The headquarters of the SNU is at Stanstead Hall, Stansted Mountfitchet, Essex CM24 8UD, England.

The third group is made up of smaller organisations, such as the United Spiritualists, the Corinthians and some other independent churches and centres.

It is not my purpose to influence the reader to accept one faction over another. In fact the reader must make up their own mind as to which is the more suitable for them, hopefully after making in-depth enquiries.

Yes, you can be a medium without joining any group, but there seems to be a trend towards certification. This has already happened with healers and I feel certain that it will eventually come for mediumship. It is the only way to improve standards.

Church services follow a fairly common routine. The main difference may be the reciting or singing the Lord's Prayer. Some churches/centres do and others do not. It really comes down to what the spiritualist group or church committee decide. To provide the reader with some idea of a spiritualist service, the following information is given only as a guide:

1. The chairperson introduces the medium(s).
2. The medium opens the service with a prayer or invocation.
3. A hymn is sung.

4. The medium gives a reading, which may be a spiritual work, a poem or a reading from the bible.
5. A hymn is sung.
6. The medium gives an address (talk or sermon). This may be inspirational or in trance.
7. A hymn is sung.
8. The medium demonstrates clairvoyance, clairsentience or clairaudience.
9. The service is concluded with a prayer.

Within nearly every church that I have visited, an atmosphere of friendliness pervades. In many churches, someone actually welcomes each person who enters. Churches quite often have other activities. These can include healing, demonstrations of mediumship and development circles. These subjects are covered elsewhere in this book.

Centres are run along similar lines and may be situated in local community centres or other such places. Quite often, instead of hymns, popular songs that have a spiritual theme are often sung.

Most churches recognise that not everybody can present a reading, an address and demonstrate mediumship; therefore some mediums work together to take a service. Some churches only accept one medium to take a service, which is a pity as it precludes two people who could offer an excellent service. It should be noted that the majority of mediums are quite capable of taking a service alone, but at times will share a service or demonstration with another equally competent medium.

Many people will not set foot into a spiritualist church or centre, mainly because someone has instilled a preconceived notion that the members are part of an illegal or unacceptable sect. There still seems to be a misunderstanding about what spiritualists are. For some reason there are assumptions that we are into witchcraft and devil worship and other such generally unacceptable practices. This misunderstanding I have to lay at the door of Christian Priests. As with any religion, those that have the duty to guide the masses must know not only their own religion, but other religions also. Without a wider knowledge, any religious leader will be wearing blinkers. As a spiritualist minister, and without any prompting by an outside source, I have made a study of other religions so that I will have a balanced view of my fellow man, regardless of the belief that he (and she) holds.

At this point it seems a good idea to touch on the bible. This is, in the main, a book relating to things that happened a couple of thousand years ago. It was certainly in a different world to that which we inhabit now. Many of the stories (or parables) were used in exactly the way in which I am writing parts of this book. They are analogous. That is they tell a story to put across an understanding of the meaning as a comparison. I feel that they are not always a verbatim account. Some of the historical information provides evidence of what actually happened, such as healing, mediumship and physical phenomena. In some religious groups, the 'speaking in tongues' is an acceptable aspect of their beliefs.

The main difference to what a lot of ignorant people believe, with regard to spiritualism, is that we do believe in one God. This, in essence, is the same God that other religions believe in. In Christian religions, there is a personal difference in specific understanding, and that holds true in the spiritualist belief also. The main difference with some understandings is that the spiritualist God is not a vengeful God, but one who has compassion and love for all. My personal belief is that 'my' God has given us free will to do what we want—with no exception. So for those that say, "Why does God do this or that", especially with regard to war and famine, it is not God but the people of this earth that do it. We must learn to be tolerant of each other and help those that suffer. If we all learnt what we are supposed to learn, then we would have no more wars or hungry people. Regardless of belief, I feel that any person who can think, should do what they can in their own life to make life easier for themselves and everyone around them.

Think of all the wars that have been waged in the name of religion and the barbaric things that have happened. Surely now is the time to realise what we are doing to our fellow man and also the animals! We can change! But will we?

CHAPTER 20

PUBLICATIONS

Some churches and centres have a library, where books are both for sale and rent. Mediums have written their biographies, and these can be interesting from the point of view of how individual mediums work. Doris Stokes, Stephen O'Brien, Doris Collins and Michael Bentine are popular names that spring to mind. Many other works, such as those by White Eagle, and Gordon Higginson, together with works by some of the founders of modern spiritualism are certainly worth reading.

There are other publications that are published in the United Kingdom on a weekly and monthly basis.

The following books are suggested as good reading, under the subject heading, together with the title, author and publisher. The reason that they are given is to provide more information to the seeker. It is not a 'must read' list. As with anything the readers will have their own choice.

| Astrology | The Compleat Astrologer | Derek & Julia Parker | Mitchell Beazley |
| Biorythms | Biorythms | Peter West | Thorsons |

Breathing	The Tao of Natural Breathing	Dennis Lewis	Redmell Press
Clairvoyance	How to develop Cl.	W E Butler	Aquarian
Communication with the Spirit World		Johannes Greber	John Felsberg Inc.
Dreams	Book of Dreams	Margarete Ward	Thorsons
Healing	The way of Absent Healing	Harry Edwards	SAGB
Herbs	The magic Healers	Paul Twitchell	IWP
Meditation	A basic course		Atlanteans
Mediumship	A Guide for Development	Harry Edwards	SAGB
Numerology	Numerology	Mary Anderson	Aquarian
Palmistry	Practical Lifelines	David Brendan-Jones	Rider
Palmistry	Life Lines	Peter West	Aquarian
Psychic	How to develop and use	Ted Andrews	Llewellyn
Reflexology	Reflexology	Anna Kaye	Thorsons

Religion	The Rock of Truth	Arthur Findlay	Psychic Press
Religion	Psychic Influences in World Religion	James F Malcolm	SNU
Remedies	Bach Flower Remedies	Julian Barnard	C W Daniel
Shiatzu	Shiatzu	Yukiko Irwin	RKP
Shiatzu	The Natural Healers Accupressure Handbook	Michael Blate	RKP
Spirit	Communication	William T Stead	Greater World
Visualisation	Creative Visualisation	Ronald Shone	Thorsons

From time-to-time there are some good CD's available. I have included some as a reference only.

Yog and Pranayam. DVD available from: Garg Enterprises 4574/15 Padamsingh Marg Daryaganj, Opposite Happy School, Delhi2, India. E-mail: gargent@bol.net.in

Breathing	Healthy Breathing	Ken Cohen

CHAPTER 21

OTHER RELIGIONS

You may think: 'Why do we wish to know about other religions?' Because I am curious, I have looked at a number of different religions with the objective of understanding my fellow man (and woman). What I found out, is that there is one theme running through just about every religion, and that is: we should be nice to each other!

Here we are in this modern world and what most of us think about is me, me, me. The spiritual way of life is essentially to serve others, although it does not seem to be so in practice. I do not find it easy to be nice to everyone, but over the years, my tolerance seems to be getting better, and I try to help where I feel able.

Where teaching is concerned, there is a need to have more knowledge than that which is being taught. How else can questions be answered if there has been no study and understanding? How can any religious leader—of whatever level—retain their congregation if there are not more answers in the leaders head than questions being voiced by students? To that end we need to know what the 'opposition' believes.

There are five main religions in this world that we live. Top of the list is **Christianity**, having about a third of the world following their beliefs. Next is **Islam** with about a fifth of the world, at number three are non-believers, having about one sixth of the world. **Hinduism** accounts for a little less and Chinese traditionalists at number 5 with about a sixteenth of the world. The next big one is **Buddhism** at number 6 with about the same following. Then come people with local beliefs, African traditional beliefs, Sikhism, Juche then comes, at number 11, Spiritists (and lumped among this belief are Spiritualists) and then *Judaism*. Obviously there are a number of other beliefs/religions, but these are the main ones.

The next step is to understand what each religion believes, and what impact it has on both the believers and those that follow another belief. Here are some religions, with a sentence or two showing that we are not that far from each other:

Christian:	Treat others the way that you wish to be treated.
Baha'i:	Do not regard what benefits you, but seek what benefits mankind.
Buddhist:	Do not hurt others in ways that you would find hurtful.
Confucianism:	The same as Christian.
Hindu:	Do nothing that you would not want done to you.
Islam:	You do not believe, until you desire for your brother the same as you desire for yourself.
Jainism:	Treat all as you wish to be treated.
Jews:	What you find hateful, do not do to others.
Sikhs:	As you see yourself, that is the way to see others.
Taoists:	Look upon your neighbour's loss as though it were your own.
Zorastians:	Do not to another that which you would not do to yourself.

It then comes as a surprise as to why there are wars. Let us look at the largest group, The Christians. What started out as followers of Christ has become something quite different. If we go back a long way, there were mediums that were called 'oracles' and there were a number of them. They foretold the future for individuals and 'world' leaders. They gave guidance for all sorts of situations. The church workers then gave the prophesies to the world at large. Eventually the church workers called themselves 'priests' and got rid of the mediums. The priests then gave information to the masses, not as a spirit communication, but as a political statement. They made their own laws.

The Sunni's and Shia's, although they are very close from a religious point of view, they seem to be miles apart with their hatred coming between them. What I do not understand is why, when they are living together in their own lands, there is so much hatred, and when they live elsewhere they can live together fairly reasonably. All over this world there is enmity; between the North and South of Ireland (although this may not only be a religious enmity); between the Pakistan and Indian peoples; between the North and South Koreans; Christians and Spiritualists, and so it goes on.

What can we do to stop the violence and killing? The only thing that I can do on a personal level is to treat all with whom I come into contact, exactly the same. I have no personal vendetta, I have respect for other religions, and I believe that sometimes we have to have rules to govern us, but that they have to be for the majority. I do not have a problem with fundamentalists in general, but when they attack other religions, saying that theirs is the only true religion, it is an invitation to enmity, and that I deplore.

We can all live in this world quite comfortably. It just takes the leaders to do what the majority of people want. Peace. The hippies had a good phrase 'make love, not war'. If only we could approach that sentiment. In a practical sense, if all church leaders studied four other religions, took on board their aims and beliefs, and spoke to their congregations about living together peacefully, I am sure there would be a much better understanding around the world.

CHAPTER 22

TRANSITIONS

A transition is when a person living in this world 'dies', then goes to the spirit world. It is going to happen to every one of us. There is no get-out clause. The only variation is when, and over that we have no choice, except by suicide and murder. As I find the last two unacceptable conditions, I will ignore them. There are a number of stages of viewing this transition. One is from the person who is taking the transition; one is from the people who are watching the transition, both from the immediate vicinity and those in the spirit world, and yet another is what planning (if any) that we do about it.

Many people know that they are getting close to leaving this earth, through the advent of old age or because they have an illness from which they will not recover. The others, unfortunately, do not have any idea when their transition will be. I say unfortunately, because there are many who do not prepare for death. We prepare ourselves in so many ways in this life, for education, work, sport, family life, having children and so on, but we, in the main, do not prepare for death as we do not think that it is going to happen to us, at least, not yet. Personally, I think that we are being a little selfish by not planning our death, and the reason that I maintain that, is because I have seen so many relatives who have to try and organise a funeral without knowing the wishes of the deceased, and also trying to carry out the organising while being in shock with their grieving.

I have my funeral completed except for the things that I do not know, such as when (although, in my mind the date of 22nd August 2022 at 10pm seems as good as any), who will actually take the service (I may outlive the choices that I have nominated), and what others may want to say. It did seem strange when I first started to put my thoughts together, but it is not much different in approach to making a will—and that is something else we should all do. I have provided a specimen of my funeral arrangements, not to be morbid in any way, but to provide some information for the thought for others. Whether a relative or not, the person who has to arrange a funeral may find the whole concept too difficult. Often I hear the comment that nobody knows what music the deceased liked, or even what their beliefs were. There are times when there are no relatives and also no friends. What a shame.

As human beings, we tend not to tell everyone what our likes and dislikes are, and in situations where we do, we may outlive those that we have told. Planning really is a must. I have had occasion to be at the hospital bedside of a friend who was very clear in her mind what she wanted as regards her service, and what words she wanted me to say on her behalf. Needless to say I carried out all that she asked. With the same lady, when I saw her next, in a hospice, she was not conscious and her family were grieving around her. It may seem blunt, but I suggested that they tell her that they gave their permission that she could go, and did not have to remain with them. An hour later she passed away. Some people who are close to passing need to know—even if it is only through their sub-conscious—that they have your permission to go.

Some people think that our death is pre-planned before we are born. It may be so, but many other aspects also come into play, such as how others impact on another's death, depending on their closeness, and what they did or did not do prior to the point of departure. When I think of all the planning by spirit that must go on in those circumstances,

I for one could not plan it so well—not even close! As a medium, we have to try and cope with the varied emotions that are prevalent, and we need to add counselling skills to our job.

Many mediums, whether ordained ministers or not, are asked to carry out a funeral service. Although, in the first instance, there is much trepidation, think of it as an honour that someone trusts you enough to carry out their last wishes. It is a service that you only have one attempt at, so it has to be right. With help, you can do it. First of all, if you are meeting the person before their transition, keep it on a part friendly and part business arrangement. I have found that even when someone knows that they are shortly to die, they often still have a sense of humour. If they laugh, it takes their mind off the subject a little, but all of the information that is required must be ascertained.

I have made up a pro-forma for funerals to assist taking information. This can be used either with the actual person or with the relatives afterwards.

FUNERAL/CREMATORIUM SERVICE/CEREMONY

Funeral Director...
Contact..
Location of service...
Date of service..
Time of service...

Deceased's name...
Known as .... Age ....
Date of passing...
Location of passing...

Family contact...
Relationship ....
Telephone number ....
Address..
....

OPENING WORDS

Tribute
Committal
Closing words

Songs/Hymns
     Entrance...
     2   ....
     3   ....
     4   ....
     Exit..

Relatives to be mentioned ....
....
....
....

Tributes by ....
....

Notes ....
....
....
....
....

Meeting with organiser..

Procession Yes/No Flower placing Yes/No Curtains Yes/No CD's

Cross left/removed Clerical Collar Yes/No Prayers Yes/No   Flowers

To explain how it works, I will take each section individually. To start with, is it a burial or a cremation? You will need to know which funeral director and who your contact is, including their 'phone number. Next comes the location, date and time of the funeral. This information is usually provided by the funeral director on a piece of pre-printed paper, although in this modern age, I now get e-mails. Next comes the information about the deceased. It is important to have the full name of the person AND the name that they were known by. The funeral director will also provide the person's age, together with information about their passing.

The next piece of information is vital. The family contact, what their relationship is to the deceased, their 'phone number and address. It is imperative to ensure that the address that you use is the right one, as often there will be given the deceased's address, which may be irrelevant to you, as you need to know where you will be meeting the contact for further information. Often there are two contacts as the obvious one (the spouse) may not be able to cope, and has delegated another member of family. Add to that, if there are two or three funerals to organise within a couple of days, mistakes can be made!

Personally, I believe that the service can be broken down into four broad areas, Opening Words, Tributes, Committal and Closing Words. Within that structure can be three or four pieces of music or hymns. There seems to be more of a need for a non-religious service with prayers and now-and-again hymns. Although it does seem to be a bit of a mixture, my job—as I see it—is to do what is wanted. I always mention those who are left behind, so it is necessary to ensure that the names and their relationship is correct. Not everyone is capable of providing a tribute or eulogy, so I offer three choices: let them do it; let them try, but I have a copy of what they are going to say so that I can pick up if they falter; or I will read anything on anyone's behalf.

Here again, I suggest that preparation is paramount. On one of my first services I was given a piece of paper to be read on someone else's behalf. This was immediately before the service, so I quickly looked at the paper, saw that it was typewritten and accepted it. Although the words that were included were not blasphemous, they caused me a little discomfort when I got to a certain phrase. I had just read them as they were on the page, but having been committed to the flow, I had no choice but to go on. In retrospect, it would have been far better to have read the text beforehand and slightly changed the words. It is a lesson that I cannot forget even though the words did provoke a laugh from everyone.

When people want to give a tribute, it is only common sense to ask in which order should the people speak. Additionally, I ask if someone could give me a potted history of the deceased, as with the best will in the world, I could never give a coherent talk about their life. Again, if there are a number of funerals to plan, it makes sense to have the date and time that the organiser will see me on the same piece of paper. There are a few items that I use as a 'tick off', these include whether the family will follow the coffin in procession into the chapel, would anyone like to place an individual flower on the coffin immediately prior to the committal, should the curtains be closed (or whatever variation), if there is a crucifix at the front of the chapel should it be removed (I have done so for Buddhist funerals), should I wear my clerical collar, should there be prayers and should that include the Lord's Prayer, is the music on a CD, tape or played on the organ. Note: tapes are not generally used now. All this is preparation when meeting the relatives or the person organising the funeral.

A burial is usually much shorter, there usually being no music played and also the weather can be adverse, although the principle is the same.

Having arranged the meeting, I usually start with talking about what music would be required. It breaks the ice and has the advantage that it is a necessary piece of information. In the case—as sometimes happens—when the organiser(s) are either not bothered or have no idea, I usually suggest light music played on the organ for the entry and exit music, and directly after the committal I suggest the organ playing Cavatina (theme from the Deerhunter). Usually, CD's are needed to be with the funeral director a day or two before the funeral.

I then move on to the 'tick offs'. In addition, I suggest that any flowers that are appropriate could be taken home as a memory of the deceased. Previously, it was suggested by others that flowers go to a hospital, but there is a tendency not to do that because they are not allowed, sometimes they can go to a hospice, but as the patients know where the flowers have come from and they do not want to be reminded of their own closeness to death, although some hospices use the flowers for therapy, by making table decorations with them.

Gently moving through the pro-forma, I fill it all in, and when I have got most of it together, I then go through the whole service order. When all information has been noted, I then go through it all again, and if required I will write it out on a separate piece of paper that I already have. I do not go through every word, as it not necessary. The whole procedure takes me about an hour. If a service sheet is required, they will have your written order of service, and the printing can usually be carried out through the help of the funeral director.

Once all the information is assembled back home on the computer, it will look something like this. I use a fictitious service purely as an illustration. The first page—the running order—is printed twice, one for me and one for the organist, so that we both know what we are doing.

Page 1

FUNERAL OF xx(name)xx
Xnd XXXXXXXXX 20XX @ XX:XX (date and time)

ORDER OF SERVICE

Procession
CD
When the Saints come marching in

Opening Address—(Officiant)

Tributes

Organ or CD
Whiter shade of pale

Committal

CD—Time to say goodbye

Closing Words—(Officiant)

Leaving
CD—Wish me luck as you wave me goodbye

Page 2

FUNERAL OF xx(name)xx
Xnd XXXXXXXXX 20XX @ XX:XX (date and time)

OPENING WORDS

We meet here today to give thanks for the life of xx(name)xx, and to express our love and admiration for him, and to bring some comfort to his family and friends, some of who are here. xx(name)xx was x(age)x. He leaves his wife, xxx, daughters xxx and xxx, son, xxx, together with many grandchildren and great-grandchildren.

We are all concerned, directly or indirectly, with the death of an individual, for we are all members of one human community. Though some of the links between us are strong and some are tenuous, each of us is joined to all the others, by links of kinship, love or friendship: by living in the same neighbourhood or town or country; or simply by our common spirituality.

The separateness, the uniqueness of each human life is the basis of our grief in bereavement. Look through the whole world, and there is no one like the one that you have lost. But he still lives on in your memories, and, though no longer a visible part of your lives, he will always remain a member of your family or circle, through the influence he has had on you and the special part that he has played in your lives.

Looking beyond our grief today, we rejoice that xx(name)xx was, and is, a part of our lives. His influence endures in the unending consequences that flow from his character and the things that he did. We shall remember him as a living vital presence. The memory will bring refreshment to our hearts in times of trouble—and maybe a few smiles.

Some words by Henry Scott Holland (1847-1918):

Death is nothing at all. I have only slipped away into the next room. I am I, and you are you. Whatever we were to each other that we are still. Call me by my old familiar name; speak to me in the easy way that you always used. Put no difference in your tone; wear no false air of solemnity or sorrow. Laugh as we always laughed at little jokes we enjoyed together. Let my name be ever the household word that it always was. Let it be spoken without an effort, without the ghost of a shadow on it.

Life means all that it ever meant. It is the same as ever it was; there is absolutely unbroken continuity. What is death but a negligible accident? Why should I be out of mind because I am out of sight? I am waiting for you, for an interval, somewhere very near, just around the corner.

All is well.

Potted History:

Other Tributes:

We will now listen to a piece of music entitled 'Whiter shade of pale'.

Please stand for the committal

Press button **(to close curtains)**

And so death has come to our friend and loved one. Here in this last rite, we commit xx(name)xx's body to its natural end. He will be part of our life for all time; through the warmth of the Summer and the cold of the Winter; through the freshness of Spring and the mists of Autumn. He will be at peace.

Please be seated

Another piece of music 'Time to say goodbye'. During this time, I would ask those of you with a religious belief to send your prayers for xx(name)xx, and for everyone else, remember in these moments all your pleasant times together.

CLOSING WORDS

With apologies to Bishop Brent.

What is dying? A ship sails and I stand watching 'til he fades on the horizon, and someone says, "He is gone." Gone where? Gone from my sight, that is all; he is just as large as when I saw him last. The diminished size and total loss of sight is in me, not in him, and just at the moment that someone says "He is gone." there are others who are watching him coming, and voices take up the glad shout, "There he comes!" . . . and that is dying.

I know that xx(name)xx would not have wanted you to go about speaking of him in whispers or in tones of false sentimentality. You are obviously aware of his sense of humour from the choice of music. He would have been amused rather than anything else at the inevitable mistakes we shall all make in still speaking of him in the present tense. He would have understood that we have to learn to speak of him in the past tense, have to adjust to thinking of the family circle without him, and he would not have found such adjustment any easier than you.

Do not be embarrassed by tears, your own or anyone else's, or suppose that an impassive face hides an unfeeling heart. Do not be concerned if grief takes you by surprise weeks after you thought it had let go of you. Do not be puzzled if the process of adjustment takes months rather than weeks. You will always have your tender memories.

I would like to thank everyone who has come here today. I hope, that as we close this farewell ceremony for xx(name)xx, you will feel glad that you had the courage to do some of your grieving in the presence of those who have suffered most, and that you have derived some comfort from gathering here.

End of service

This service has taken me some time to get to this state and I have used the format many times, with a few changes. Hopefully it will help those who are asked to take a service.

There are different poems and words that can be used, and much can be found on the internet. I find that as there are so many differences between people, that some words/poems are appropriate and some are not.

Additional verses
(These need to be changed for male/female)

Let us pray:

O God, our Father, who holdeth all good things in Thy safe keeping, we pray for our sister who has completed her earthly span. We thank thee for all that she accomplished, and now that sickness and sorrow are no more, and death is past, that she lives forever in thy love and care.
 Amen.

Father of mercies and God of all comfort, look in thy tender love and pity, we beseech thee, on thy sorrowing servants. We commend to your tender care those who mourn the loss of a loved one. Give them the peace that passes all understanding, and let them know that neither death nor life can separate them from your love.
 Amen.

We will all say together the Lord's Prayer

Our Father, who art in heaven, Hallowed be thy name;
Thy kingdom come; Thy will be done;
On earth as it is in heaven. Give us this day our daily bread.
And forgive us our trespasses,
As we forgive those that trespass against us.
And lead us not into temptation;
But deliver us from evil.

For thine is the kingdom, the power, and the glory,
For ever and ever. Amen.

There are a few items that may need addressing, such as using the microphone. I speak fairly softly, so I ensure that the microphone is closer to me, especially if my text is on the lectern and my head is lowered. I try and speak clearly, with a few pauses. There is nothing worse than listening to someone steaming through the words. Usually they are inaudible and it gives a feeling of the service being rushed. This I will not do. Before the actual service, I ensure the length of time that I have to carry out the service. I usually take between 20 and 35 minutes, this in a slot of 45 minutes.

At the end, prior to the mourners leaving, I go to the principle mourners and tell them to take their time and which door to leave from. Some like to stop and listen to the last piece of music before leaving. I will not rush them.

You may well be asked to join the mourners if they gather elsewhere. Whatever you do, remember that their emotions are still raw.

Note: Some crematoria have half hour slots others have different timings. This needs to be ascertained as part of the planning. Also, some crematoria have different ways of playing music, such as pressing buttons in a certain order. It always pays to check.

As with all things, my funeral service may change over time, as I change my mind! Also, there are many poems that are being written by all sorts of people. They are maybe worth considering

CHAPTER 23

QUESTIONS AND ANSWERS

There are many questions that may require an answer. To that end a number of questions were obtained by asking many different people to provide 'their' question. The questions are given together with an answer, located under a number of collective headings.

The purpose of life,
What happens at death?
Life after death,
Communication between the two worlds,
Spirit guides angels and guardian souls,
      The spiritual hierarchy,
      The nature of God,
Spiritual healing,
Development of spiritualism,
Prayer,
Religion,
Auras,
Psychic and mediumistic development, and
Reincarnation.

THE PURPOSE OF LIFE

Q!   Why do disabled people seem to be good at painting and other similar gifts?

A1   Because some people have a disability, it does not mean that they are shut off from spiritual progression. Each of us has to have an outlet to show that there is something inside of us that is beautiful. For someone who has a beautiful face, they may not be beautiful inside, so why should someone (to outsiders) who is not beautiful, not be able to express the beauty that is inside them?

Q2   When some people are not sure of their gender, is it because they were a different gender in their previous life?

A2   We have a choice as to what difficulties we will accept in our life on earth before we return. To return to this earth with an uncertainty of our gender will give us many trials, each of which will help us in our progression. For my part, many of my friends are either gay or uncertain of their position in society, but I accept them as they are, just as they accept me as I am.

Q3   Why do the 'good' die young?

A3   It is my understanding that those who have completed all their earthly tasks will return home to the spirit world. To complete our tasks, we need to show all those aspects that make up a 'good' person. These aspects include love, compassion, understanding, tolerance, etcetera. If we have achieved all that we set out to do, then we go home.

Q4   Why do babies and children die?

A4   I will refer to the answer above. The situation is very similar. I see the early death of a child in those terms. They have come for the experience and that is all. There is no need—in a spiritual sense—for more than that. Unfortunately, this is not the concept that is experienced by those that have been left behind. The bigger picture is that we spend only a relatively short time on this earth, and forever in the spirit world—which I define as home.

Q5   If one has a transplant, what effect does it have on the recipient's body?

A5   There have been many studies of the effects on people who have had transplants from other donors, and these show that some of the donor's personality or trait is demonstrated in the recipient. There are a number of books on the subject.

Q6   If we eat meat, do we take on some aspect of that animal?

A6   As you would understand, after reading Answer 5, it is entirely consistent that it is so. I sometimes wonder about the attitude of some of the younger generation, where they tend to hunt in packs, and have a mentality geared to inter-dependency as opposed to individualism.

WHAT HAPPENS AT DEATH?

Q1   Why do groups of people annihilate other groups and what happens to both groups in the spirit world?

A1   Mostly, it is because of jealousy and greed. It's an 'I want what you have got' syndrome. When those that perpetrate such atrocities get to the spirit world they will associate with those that are like-minded, and not mix with those that have different viewpoints. Once in the spirit world there is an opportunity for them to realise their wrong thinking and wrong-doing, and if they wish they may progress to somewhere better.

Q2   What happens to people such as Hitler, when they die?

A2   They also go to the spirit world, but they are in an area where they are with their own kind. As there is progression open to every soul, the ability to atone for their sins is available. As I understand it, some good souls go to this area to offer help to those who want it. This may take a lot longer than we could ever understand.

Q3   I have heard that a person's spirit has weight. Is this true?

A3   A picture/movie was made entitled '22grams', and this represents the weight change by 22 grams of a person at death. There is information available as to how and under what circumstances the dying body was weighed. There is some speculation with regard to what actually goes, and where it goes, as there is also a thought that when we are in spirit we are weightless. Some feel that it is the soul that has weight, others that it is the mind.

Q4   If someone commits suicide, what happens to them spiritually?

A4   They do not go to purgatory! They usually go to a place similar to a hospital where they recover from their transition. Often there is a deep-rooted problem that makes someone commit suicide and there will be help awaiting them. They go to the same spiritual realms as others.

Q5   When I die, will there be someone waiting for me?

A5   I have a little difficulty with this question. My belief tells me that we are all met by someone that we know—and for those who know their guides, they may also be there. But when I think about exorcism, which is to return the earthbound spirit to the spirit world, how can this be true? It may be that only a relatively few are earthbound, put in that position by I know not what. I am fully aware that there are many people, who just before their transition, seem to be more alert and seem to speak to someone who has gone on before. This provides me with my belief that we are met.

Q6   Is it wrong to help someone to pass to the spirit world when nearly all the physical abilities have gone?

A6   This answer will change according to people's beliefs. The viewpoint is: would we not put down an animal if it is suffering, even when there may be a firmly held belief that it is wrong to do the same for a human being who is suffering. It may seem callous to suggest that we should use the same criteria, but when human emotion comes into play especially when coloured by the law of the land, most people have a great difficulty to come to a sensible conclusion. For my own part, if I were suffering and my useful life had been concluded, and there was no hope of recovery then I would like to leave this earthly life—especially when I consider the state of the world as it is at this moment.

Life After Death

Q1   What is the spirit world?

A1   The spirit world is 'home'. It is the place from where we come and also the place where we return when we die, in the earthly sense. It gives a realisation that there is no death, but continuation of life, although maybe not as we know it on this earth plane.

Q2   Where is the spirit world?

A2   The spirit world is where spirits are. When we die we go to the spirit world, but without confines of space. As we progress, we are able to be anywhere we wish to be just by the power of thought, and in that time. This does not mean that spirit is at our beck and call as they have other things to do, such as learning and helping in areas of difficulty that we have in this world or elsewhere.

Q3   I have heard it said that there are seven levels in the spirit world. Is this true?

A3   Certainly it is true that we can progress during the time that we spend in the spirit world. There have been many statements that there are seven levels, but I cannot see that we have to achieve something specific to move to the next level, although I can accept that there is a fluid progression, just as there is in this earthly life.

Q4   My loved one is in the spirit world, but I have not had any communication. Have they gone somewhere else?

A4   One of the problems with communication from the spirit world is that some of the people who are expected to 'come through' are waiting for the right medium. This may seem a little bit suspect, but a well-known medium was taking a workshop in Paignton, Devon, and asked a pupil to give a message to him. This is an accepted way to judge whether a communication is correct or not. The student (who happens to be my wife) gave some evidence to him that was unique and quite correct. He had waited over 20 years for that message, but the person in the spirit world had waited until the medium that gave the message, was the right one. Maybe it was another lesson from our spirit friends.

There comes a time, I feel, when the ties of a person in the spirit world becomes somewhat looser. I am aware that we have the opportunity to progress further in the spirit world, and with both of those thoughts, it would be logical that the need to communicate may diminish. It does not mean that those of us on the earth do not have a need, but if you look at it from a spiritual, and spirit world point of view, they will be seeing us in a relatively short time, so the need on their part may be lessened.

Q5   If we live on the planet earth now, can we exist somewhere else in another existence?

A5   Much has been said about being in more than one place at a time, but the best way of understanding is to relate to how we are, here and now. Although we take up the finite amount of space that we have while we are here, we can also radiate our being anywhere, and that will give the impression that we are in more than one place at a time.

COMMUNICATION BETWEEN TWO WORLDS

Q1   Where can I find a reputable medium?

A1   If I were facetious, I would probably say "with great difficulty". There is only one way that is worth while, and that is by recommendation only. Over the years, I have been to many mediums—some of international fame—and have been disappointed. I now wait until I hear of someone who really shines, then listen to what others say who I can trust, and then maybe have a reading. It is well known that some mediums that demonstrate their mediumship at large venues may not be able to give a good one-to-one reading, and vice versa.

     I maintain that those who advertise need people to go to them, whereas those who are good and do not advertise, generally are more worthwhile. With regard to costs, just because a medium charges a lot of money does not guarantee a good reading! Often the reverse can be true.

Q2   How does mediumship work?

A2   Very much like a television or radio. Those who are mediumistic tune in to sights and sounds known as clairvoyance and clairaudience. Additionally there is clairsentience, which is the sensing side of our abilities. There are some in the spirit world who transmit the sights, sounds and senses for us to pick up, just like television or radio. We have to be attuned to receive the transmissions. Apart from a lucky few who are born with these abilities, the rest of us have to sit in a development circle—sometimes for many years.

Q3   Why does a guide work with a medium?

A3   There are many on this earthly plane that wish to help others without a need either to be recognised or to be paid. This comes from an inherent desire to do good. This is equally so in the spirit world. Looking at the consideration of time, spiritual guides would not see that they would do this job forever, although there does seem to be some evidence of a bond between a guide and a person who is living to go on beyond the grave. I am aware of bonds being forged in the spirit world between two people who both reside in the spirit world. When one of them is incarnated, the other can be the main guide.

Others in the spirit world will join a person's guide to learn how to do the work. This then gives us understanding that not all guides know everything, and that there are differing levels of knowledge. If we were to go to the spirit world and take up a position as a person's guide, how would we cope without quite intensive training?

Q4   Does everyone have a guide?

A4   Yes, but that does not mean everyone is aware or even interested in having a guide. From time to time, even the most disinterested of us will do things that may be out of character for someone else's good. Where does this come from? Our guide. As we progress along a spiritual path—and this is not necessarily spiritualism—we then have more guides who have different abilities to enable us to become better in various areas of spiritual development.

Q5   I have been asked by friends to take part in a ouija board sitting. Should I?

A5   The short answer is NO! Having said that, there are sometimes circumstances where it can work without causing harm. This is when the person in control is a competent medium, and is strict in the way that the session is conducted. I often wonder why people want to use this sort of communication. It can be likened to using a very old basic typewriter, when we are in the age of computers. Why 'play' with an ouija board when spirit communication through clairaudience, clairsentience and clairvoyance is available? OK, not everybody can do it well, but it is a lot easier than spelling out words with an entity, that at worst, could cause the individuals' harm or even death.

Q6   When people use either Tarot or Palmistry; do they contact the spirit world?

A6   The short answer (again) is NO! This does not mean that a mixing of divination tools such as Tarot and Palmistry (and runes and tea leaves, etc.) and proper mediumship cannot provide a more rounded reading, especially if the problems are to do with material aspects. The use of a divination tool, together with mediumship and attunement with the individual (often referred to as the Querant) can give a very clear answer to a person with material problems.

Q7   What is direct voice?

A7   It is a voice from the spirit world that is not connected to any person living. It is usually through a voice box that is made from ectoplasm and external to the medium that is being used.

Q8   What is ectoplasm?

A8   Ectoplasm is moisture and mucus from the body, which is used by spirit to mould forms of spirit people either as a complete entity or as a part. Most of it comes from the medium. If it is touched it can cause damage to the medium. This is why sitters are warned not to touch anything (because séances are usually carried out in the dark). It is fine if the ectoplasm/spirit form touches a person, as sometimes they even shake hands.

Once, in our séance, a sitter tried to touch the ectoplasm and it immediately pulled back into the medium's body. This caused great deal of pain to the medium, and the bruises showed for a couple of weeks afterwards. In this case, I immediately closed the session, got rid of the sitters and attended the medium. The person who admitted trying to touch the ectoplasm was banned. They were our friends, but are not now.

Q9   What is transfiguration?

A9   It is the sight of another person's features superimposed on the sitter's face. There are two levels. The first is where the transfiguration can only be seen clairvoyantly, and the other is where every person who is watching will see it. Obviously the second is the more acceptable way as it contains more proof. Unfortunately for those less gifted, when mediums can see transfiguration and a few do not, then doubt is prevalent.

Q10   Are there different levels of trance?

A10   Yes. In 'the old days' trance was presumed to mean that the person sitting (medium) would be completely unaware of what transpired. Nowadays, the level of trance can be much lighter, so much so that the medium will hear everything that is going on and question themselves as to whether they are doing it right. It is a difficulty that should be endured, as there is now no real need for deep trance for every occasion.

Q11   Is it dangerous to become involved with the spirit world?

A11   As with anything, provided that the rules are followed, then no, but who nowadays cares about rules. This is my main worry. If we consider the differing types of people who go to the spirit world, there are some who we would not associate with if they were on the earth. If we are sensible, and do what a competent medium teaches us, then no harm will normally arise. As with anything, common sense rules.

There are times when we are tested though. My wife and I have been under a psychic attack, and it is far from pleasant! We think that it was initiated from somebody living on the earth, but the attack happened very physically, without anyone living being present. I do not say this with the hope that you will become alarmed; rather, it is an acceptance that sometimes things go wrong when they are not expected. For most people this will never happen.

If we each learn our lessons correctly, under the guidance of a medium that really knows what they are doing, then the spirit world is a very safe place, with many friends there who will give us help when we really need it.

Q12   It seems that England is the centre of spiritualism. Are other countries as far advanced?

A12   As with anything, change happens. England, or more correctly, the United Kingdom, has been at the forefront of spiritualism and its spiritual studies for many years. For some reason the quality of mediumship has generally deteriorated, even though there are many well-established venues that teach spiritualism and associated studies. I think that it is not the fault of those who are teaching, but those who are being taught. There is a more 'instant acquirement' required nowadays. The basics have not been absorbed enough and fledglings want to fly before their wings have developed properly.

I teach in Denmark and find that the countries that have a lack of acceptable resources contain people who really want to learn properly. I found the same in the Netherlands, Germany and Spain. I look at America in a similar way to the UK. The quality of mediumship is not generally at a good enough level, at the places where my wife and I have been. From what we have seen, true mediumship has only demonstrated by special people such as James van Praagh and John Edward. At venues that we have attended the level is more on the psychic.

Q13   What is automatic writing?

A13   When a person is entranced, spirit can and do guide the person's hand to write. Again, the level of trance may vary considerably. I have witnessed a person who is unaware of what is happening that would have a pen or pencil placed in their hands and write (and draw) on the piece of paper, stop, then continue when a new piece of paper was presented. It is a good idea to use smooth wallpaper, writing on the plain side, with a couple of people to wind the paper out and in.

Psychic artists use the same method, except that they are, in the main, fully aware of what is transpiring around them. There are times when famous artists from the past are willing to guide the hand of the writer/drawer.

Q14   I have heard that in a physical circle that holes can appear in our clothes. Is this true?

A14   Yes. This is why I ask my students to wear the same clothes at each meeting (suitably washed, of course). A lot of energy is used, and some material is lost in the process.

Q15   Is it possible to visit the spirit world while living in this material life, and how can it be done?

A15   When we are in an altered state, such as during sleep or trance, we can and do associate with others, either in the spirit world or others who are in the sleep or trance state. This includes both the spirit and earth worlds.

Q16   What is the mirror of the mind?

A16   The mirror of the mind is a way of expressing a way of receiving spiritual impressions that do not come with natural thought. A way of explaining this is, when I allow spirit to talk through me in a very slightly altered state; I am also listening to what is being said. The problem that I have in that state, is starting to think about what is being said, thus interrupting the flow of information. The information does not go through the normal thinking process, but impresses on 'the mirror of the mind', bypassing natural thought.

SPIRIT GUIDES, ANGELS & GUARDIAN SOULS

Q1   I understand that a number of guides control a physical circle. What happens to my own guides when I attend a physical circle?

A1   Over the years, I have come to the conclusion that in a well-run circle, there is a main coordinator in the spirit world. All of the people sitting in a circle 'bring' their own guides and they work together for the benefit of all. This is so with all the different types of circle. With a physical circle, the main guide of the physical medium sometimes controls all that happens sometimes someone is specially designated. As the leader of a physical circle, my guides blend with those of the medium to assist where possible. They tell me what is going on in the background, and also what I need to do in a physical sense. Other sitter's guides are generally not doing too much, depending upon the individual's development, because apart from giving energy, it becomes a situation where the sitters are just aware of what is happening with some interaction.

Q2   What is an Angel? Are they the same as spirit guides?

A2   My understanding is that our friends in the spirit world have the ability to progress spiritually, and those that have achieved more than others become Angels. Angels are here to help with stabilising this world by influencing people in this world, but as we all have free will, they have a difficult job.

Q3   Do guides still learn in the spirit world?

A3   Yes. Life in the spirit world is not a case for putting your feet up and relaxing. It is a place of progression, once we have gone past the point of getting used to our new environment. All knowledge is available. When a person dies, they can if they so wish, become a guide for a certain person on our earthly world. It now becomes obvious that we cannot suddenly acquire the skills to do this job, so another who does have the skills teaches us. In fact a partnership is forged between the 'new' medium and their spirit guide. They both learn together with the help of a teacher/medium and a guide with their tutor.

Q4   When a person is entranced, can guides speak in any language?

A4   This is an area where there are conflicting views. My belief is yes, they can speak in other, unknown languages. Some people say that the mind of the medium is used, and that only information in that medium's mind can be used. I refute this. I have witnessed things that could never be in a person's mind and things have happened that surpass the individual's intelligence.

I am aware of a person who was deeply entranced, who had no knowledge of foreign languages, speaking in a number of different languages at a gathering, where the person had only gone to witness another medium. The person was entranced without ever having done so before.

Q5   Do guides know everything?

A5   In my opinion, no. Each person who goes to the spirit world does not suddenly become all-knowing. We are also aware that the personality that we have on this earth is taken with us to the spirit world. Some of us are very opinionated, and think that we know most things—if not everything, when the truth is very different. If we go to the spirit world with this understanding, what answer would we provide for our medium who asks us a question about anything that we would normally have little or no knowledge of?

Q6   What do guides think about capital punishment?

A6   Capital punishment is murder in another form and therefore not acceptable.

Q7   What is spirit's opinion of gaols (jails)? Is there a better way?

A7   There is always a better way, but in the light of the development of the human race, it cannot be implemented at this time. What we should be doing is to educate everyone sufficiently well with regard to morality for them not to need imprisonment.

Q8   Do we have more than one guide?

A8   If we regard life as a classroom, and then relate that to our abilities and what we want to do, then we will either have one or many guides. It really does depend on whether the individual wants to work with spirit a little bit or a lot. It is generally accepted that we all have one guide who is our 'door keeper', the person who looks after our interests. It does not mean that we have someone in spirit stopping any problems for us though. They often allow things to happen that we do not want, because it is required for the growth of our soul.

Q9   What should my attitude be to my guide(s)?

A9   The best way that I can answer this is, what do you do as you forge a friendship with someone who becomes your very best friend? You will not know in the beginning whether it will turn out as you expect, but you will be hopeful. Therefore, you will probably want to project and maintain your very best side. You will want to be courteous and understanding. If you provide this honest aspect then you will more than likely have it returned in full measure.

Q10   Are we allowed to laugh with mediumship?

A10   If it is wrong, then I, and those who have walked this path with me, have made a real mess of it. Laughter really brings up the vibrations and those in the spirit world love a laugh as much as we. This is laughing WITH mediumship, not at it.

Q11   Are spirits a higher intelligence than us?

A11   To answer with a question—on this earthly world, are there others with a higher intelligence than us? As we progress through our incarnation, not only do we have more knowledge, but also, hopefully, we increase our awareness of what is the right thing to do in differing circumstances. We are in the spirit world for a very long time compared with living on this earth, so we should acquire more tolerance and understanding. On the other hand do we mean a higher intelligence or do we mean a higher awareness and understanding?

Q12   What is spirit's opinion of marriage and divorce?

A12   Marriage and divorce are man-made situations, not spiritual. The aspects that anyone who wishes to aspire to the highest ideals, are constancy, love, tolerance, understanding and so on. Marriage and divorce are not present in the spirit world. If you were married and they were the love of your life and that was reciprocated, then you will be together again, if not you could meet on a friendship level, otherwise you would not necessarily meet ever again.

Q13   Do spirits actually see us?

A13   I have a little difficulty with this question. My considered answer is that spirit are very aware of us if they want to be. I do not think that they can actually SEE us, as we understand the word. Please do not be fearful that all our intimate and private acts are watched with a critical eye! I am aware that many things can be sensed, as we sense things, but I feel that the spirit beings are just a bit more sensitive than us.

Q14   Can spirits move our possessions?

A14   Yes. Having been a party to five and ten pound notes suddenly disappearing, and then at a later time to let us know that they are around, spirit actually gives us one pence pieces that are bright and shiny. It is a pity that it's not the other way around. My wife and I have had apports from spirit. Mine was an RAF cap badge (I was in the Royal Air Force); my wife's apport was very hot when it was put into her hand. Spirit told her to just hold it until it had cooled. It turned out to be a stone. Both of these were given in a séance at different times.

Many people have had various things moved in their house, so although not an everyday occurrence, it is quite common.

The Spiritual Heirarchy

Q1   Why are spiritual guides only North American Natives and Chinese?

A1   They are not. I am aware of guides being other races and one that is close was a child flower seller in London. She is six and three quarters and a bit, dresses in a nurse's uniform and helps a spirit doctor by giving injections. I have witnessed the injections and although there is no pain, there is a feeling of the needle entering the body. Some two hours later there is sometimes a visible indentation.

Q2   What is the Spiritual Hierarchy?

A2   Using a school as an analogy, as our knowledge and abilities increase in the spirit world, we move to a different class where we can be given even more knowledge. The ultimate aim is to become a very enlightened soul.

Q3   Why have there been different masters, such as Jesus and Buddha?

A3   Personally, I think that we are all too much taken up with our own interests to really listen to what we are being told. Maybe we are also sceptical. It then becomes logical that we have had more than one master trying to tell us that we should be nice to each other. We do not seem to be getting the message; if we did, there would not be wars.

Q4   Will there be other masters in the future?

A4   Personally, I feel that we have amongst us many who are trying to show us the way. When the masters came to this world, they were the right way to try and guide the world's populace at that time. Life was simple then, and there was also simple thought. Now we have brains that are more diverse, and we need a different way of being shown the right way to live. We now have a stronger mentality with which to dissect the information that is available. Each of us really knows right from wrong, and as we have free will we have the ability to change for the better or not. Do you at this time need someone to tell you right from wrong? Then maybe you are the master that you need.

Q5   What do spirits do in the spirit world?

A5   It is generally accepted that as soon as we die, we go to a 'rehabilitation centre', depending on how we pass over. The next stage is where we live very much as we do now. With thought we can create what we have here, and if you are happy to do so, then you can tend your garden or whatever. Eventually, there comes a need to progress, and the facilities for doing so are available.

Q6   How do spirits progress?

A6   There are halls of learning, although the concept is different to what we have here. We learn at our own pace, with no one badgering us to do better, it comes from within. Learning is not just the concept that we have in our earthly life; it is our soul that is learning.

Q7   Do animals co-exist with other spirit forms in the spirit world?

A7   As I understand it, animals that generally group together will do the same in the spirit world, such as cattle and wild animals. As there is no need for killing other animals for food, the killing aspect is redundant.

Q8   Do our family pets stay with us in the spirit world?

A8   It is my understanding that our pets who share a love bond with us do not go back to a group soul, but wait for us with someone whom we know, in the spirit world. When we arrive there, they will be there to meet us, just as before, with love and complete trust. I really am looking forward to that time.

The Nature Of God

Q1   What is natural law?

A1   Natural law is God's law. For those who seek the truth and have a need to improve their moral abilities, they will discover all of the natural laws through their conscience.

Q2   Is the Great White Spirit, God?

A2   We each have a different concept of God. If we believe in one force, one power, one infinite being, then yes we do have a similar belief. As each of us are different in our understanding of everything, then it is quite plausible that our concept of God or the Great White Spirit may have minor differences, but essentially it is the same.

    The life force that is on our planet is there, so we accept it. If we accept that God created the world, or if we accept that the world evolved, it really does not matter. We used to worship the sun as a major god, but as we evolve our concept changes, even though our basic beliefs remain the same. Within the majority of us is a need to give respect to a much greater force than ourselves. This is the basis of our belief.

Spiritual Healing

Q1   What can a healer, heal?

A1   If we accept the total intelligence of the spirit world working with a competent healer, then anything can happen. In my own case, many years ago I was diagnosed with a worn out shoulder, and the doctor then said that the other one was worse! I was put on the waiting list to have a new shoulder fitted (the worst one). In the meantime I visited Steven Turoff (a trance healer) on three different occasions. Each visit cost me 20 pounds, one for the 'best' shoulder and twice for the other. I am still pain free and have as much mobility as anyone else my age. I had to cancel the operation at the hospital, as I did not need it. I hasten to add, that others have had healing from the same source, but with no obvious benefit.

I must touch on trance healing here. My wife gave trance healing to a lady with fibroids. Her spirit doctor, Dr Rowland, carried out an operation on this lady, with the result that the operation was cancelled. The hospital had x-rays to show both before and after, but of course, they say it sorted itself out.

Q2   Where can I find a healer?

A2   In this question I assume that we are talking about a spiritual healer. There are a number of organisations that provide training to become a healer, which is now a two-year course. Once an individual becomes a certificated healer, then and only then are they let loose on the general public. If someone says that they are a healer, check their certificate and /or warrant, and if concerned even then, check with the organisation.

Apart from the various spiritual bodies that provide healing, there is also the National Federation of Spiritual Healers who have no religion in their work. All spiritual organisations that offer healing, together with the NFSH, come under the UK Healers. These can be contacted at: PO Box 4137, London W1A 6FE. E-mail: admin@ukhealers.info. Website: www. ukhealers.info

Q3   How long does healing take?

A3   Sometimes seconds, sometimes weeks. There are many variations because we are all different. I also feel that there is a special time for some people as to when they are ready for healing. Maybe we do not want a physical or mental problem, and wish to get rid of it, but we are not ready spiritually to give it up. In other words, we have not learnt the lesson that the problem is giving us.

I have had psychic surgery on my shoulders. The right shoulder was treated twice, the left, once. This was after my doctor had said to me that one shoulder was worn out and the other one was worse. This was a few years ago. I was on a waiting list for a replacement shoulder, but because I was 'cured' I cancelled the operation.

Q4   How do I know whether I can trust a healer?

A4   By ensuring that they are an accredited healer (in England we have to pass a very stringent two-year course) and also by reputation. It does not cause a problem to ensure that the healer offering their services is competent. One word of caution. Not every healer can (or should say that they can) heal everything or everybody. If someone made that claim then I would not go to them.

Q5   How does healing work?

A5   There is some slight disagreement about the source of healing, but it is generally accepted that it is from a spiritual or divine source. Some argue that it comes from nature, but to be honest, I think that the jury is still out. The important thing is—it works!

Q6   How does it work when a healer goes into trance to do psychic surgery?

A6   Trance is a word that gives an incorrect impression. A person in trance is understood to be completely unaware of what is happening. When referring to psychic surgery, it is an altered state, that is, awareness is still retained. The degree of the altered state depends on the person who is being used. It is an 'allowing' of the spirit surgeon to work through the healer, but without any real control by the healer.

Q7   Is psychic surgery safe?

A7   In general, yes, but here again caution needs to be exercised. I have been to a psychic surgeon and all pain was removed. The condition (worn out shoulders) is still there but I am able to function as well as anyone of my age. I have seen the results of a different psychic surgeon who demonstrated on my wife. She was left with much bruising. Although this was a very well known person, it is not acceptable. I have seen two other psychic surgeons working at my house who have the utmost care for their patients, and were highly successful.

Q8   Assuming that healing is good, how are thieves, murderers and suchlike, transformed?

A8   In exactly the same way as anyone else. Healing not only works on the physical body, but also on the mind and spiritual body and therefore has the ability to transform, in subtle ways, the very essence of everyone. It may take longer for some than others.

Q9   When I have healing, do I have to believe that it will work?

A9   No, but if the recipient's mind is open to healing, then there is a better condition for the healing to work.

Development Of Spirituality

Q1   There seems to be nobody in my area who can help me with my spiritual progression. Can I do it on my own?

A1   In truth yes, but I would not advise anyone to try and develop completely on their own. There are times when we can be entranced or have light control, where we may be less sure that what we are doing is acceptable. Without someone else watching over us from the material side of life, how can we be sure of our safety?

Some people that I know have been aware of spirit interest and have developed their abilities to a certain degree, but there is a need to sit with others in the control of a circle with a competent leader. None of us is totally self sufficient, and it is always prudent to ensure that all the safety aspects are in place.

Q2 When in trance, how does a guide 'take over', and where does the person go who is entranced?

A2 I cannot speak for all, as I feel that there are other aspects of which I am unaware. Having spoken at length with a limited number of people who 'go into trance', I believe that our mind is used to control all of our faculties. We do not give our bodies, as such, to the spirit world for them to operate. A friend said that he felt that he was in a warm foam-like or feather-like covering all the while he was in trance.

The personality of a spirit person is superimposed onto the mind of the person in trance. As the mind controls our actions, then it can be understood that all the subsequent actions by the entranced person will show the words and actions of the person doing the entrancing.

Q3 I want to become more spiritual. How can I do this?

A3 A big question! What is the understanding of being spiritual? Is it a way to make others make an individual more acceptable or is it to aspire to being a good person who helps others without thought of reward?

I have, over the years, tried to improve myself by being a 'better' person. This includes, helping others, being nice—even when I really do not want to be, being more tolerant, seeing the other person's point of view, and so on. When I was ordained, I realised that what I had done was not really good enough. I was told that my job was to be of service to others, so I have tried.

PRAYER

Q1 Who actually hears our prayers?

A1 Our spirit friends and guides, together with angels. These are our spirit messengers who help us.

Q2   Does anybody react to our prayers?

A2   Yes. There are times when we feel that our prayers are ignored, and I have had experience of that. We have to look at what we pray for. Is it for something that we can easily get for ourselves or is it to do with requesting help for someone who really does need spiritual help? Prayer can be selfish, but if it is for our spiritual guidance then why not. So many people ask for things that, logically, we should not. When there is a very real need, the prayers are answered, although not always in the way that we would expect.

Q3   The Lord's Prayer is mostly spoken by rote. Would sincere prayer from the heart be more effective?

A3   When I first consciously started my spiritual development I thought that a prayer from the heart would be more powerful as it would contain all the emotion and urgency that I had. Having grown older (and hopefully, wiser) I now understand the power of the Lord's Prayer. It has been used with great passion over the last 2000 years and therefore has a potency of its own. I know that it is used in times of acute trouble, and also know that it does work.

Q4   Does group prayer have more potency than one person's prayer from the heart?

A4   Of course, assuming that all of the group are praying from the heart.

Q5   How strong is prayer?

A5   Let me put it in the perspective of healing. It can change a person who is desperately ill and near to death to being fully alive. There is no limit to the power of prayer. Healing, though, can be allowing a person to go to the spirit world. It removes their pain.

RELIGION

Q1   I think that my home is 'possessed'. How can I get help?

A1   Generally, most people would go to their own priest, but there is the possibility of approaching either a reputable medium or spiritualist church. It really comes down to what is comfortable to you and also who provides the service that you require. There is no hard and fast way of coming to a specific answer. Just keep asking.

Q2   Why does the established church (Protestant & Catholic) not promote the spirit world? There are so many parallels between Jesus and spiritual beliefs.

A2   I believe that it comes down to what the hierarchy of each religion really wants to promote. Arguably, the Christian religion controls the parameters of their parishioner's beliefs, whereas spiritualists allow free thought.

Q3   What is religion?

A3   Religion is a word used by us, as groups of people, to identify who we are as regard to our beliefs. Within each group are differences in specifics, but generally they are acceptable by all in the group. Certain of the group will take one aspect and say that is their whole belief. These are fundamentalists, and are not true to the rest of the group, and often are more militant.

Q4   What should children's religious education comprise?

A4   As I see it, at this time, all children should be taught about all religions. The only way that we as a collection of nations can move forward in peace is by understanding the differences between our beliefs and accepting them. Differences without understanding cause difficulties.

Q5   Should we institute Lyceums for both children and adults?

A5 Any place that can initiate better understanding must be a good thing. Adults need education in religious tolerance just as much as children.

AURAS

Q1 What is an aura?

A1 An aura is a coloured emanation from ourselves. It can be proven using Kirlean photography, and there have been many pictures taken. Every living thing has an aura. Within the aura can be detected differing colours that can be used by knowledgeable people to check, among other things, our health.

Q2 Can anyone see an aura?

A2 Not with our normal eyesight. It usually needs a person who is mediumistic, although not all mediums can see auras.

Q3 What are chakras?

A3 These are energy centres located in parts of our body. They are often depicted as vortices or swirling energy, and in eastern religions as flowers. Each one rotates in opposition to the one that it is next to. Colours are usually apportioned to each one. They are as follows: Base of the spine, colour-red; sacral, colour-orange; solar plexus, colour-yellow; heart, colour-green; throat, colour-blue, brow, colour-indigo; crown, colour-gold or silver.

There are many books dealing with this subject. Sometimes the colours of the top two are modified. They are often grouped as lower (four) and upper (three).

Psychic And Mediumistic Development

Q1   What is a medium?

A1   A medium is a person who has abilities connected with accepting messages from the spirit world and passing them on to another person who is unable to do so.

Q2   Is a clairvoyant different to a medium?

A2   A clairvoyant is a person who sees pictures in their mind and sometimes spirit forms transmitted from the spirit world. A medium is a person who can be clairvoyant, clairaudient (hears) or clairsentient (feels).

Q3   Can I become a medium?

A3   Yes. The only person who cannot be is a person who does not want to become one. The next problem is that not all who wish to be, can become competent. We can all use our abilities, but as with any other walk of life, we cannot all become masters of our skills.

Q4   I have been invited to join a development circle. I know very little, so how can I find out if it is for me?

A4   First of all, why were you invited? Secondly, who is leading the circle, and are they both capable and competent? Thirdly, who else is sitting? Fourthly, what is the object of the circle? Once you have the answers to these questions, then you can make a decision. Usually, in a well-run circle, there is a probation time in which both the leader and yourself will be given the chance to withdraw if it is not for you.

Please refer to the section on circles in Chapter 4.

Q5   How can I protect myself from 'nasty' spirits?

A5   In a well-run circle, one of the first things that are taught is how to 'open up' and 'close down'. This is a mental way of opening your chakras to work with the spirit world and closing them when you have finished. Protection in normal circumstances is adequate when 'closing down'. For further protection, one must first consider what the problem is and then take the action required. As this is beyond the scope of this book, I suggest reading about psychic attacks and their prevention.

Q6   If I am new to an area, how can I find out where a good and honest medium is?

A6   Keep asking. You will eventually come across a medium that possibly does not advertise and is well thought of in the community. Recommendation should be the only way that you should choose. I know of one good medium who has 'phone calls from America to book a sitting (these are air hostesses flying into a major UK airport). Others travel from Cornwall and Scotland. Just because a person has a name that is well known does not guarantee a good reading.

Q7   What is a séance?

A7   A séance is where a group of people sit with a physical medium and spirit communicate in a physical way. That is by direct voice, being voices that are heard by everyone sitting, but not from anyone else except spirit. Additionally, physical materialisation can take place, which is a manifestation of a spirit person in a physical form, which can—in certain circumstances—be touched.

Q8   Why do some mediums work better with some people and not others?

A8   As in any association between people, we get on better with some rather than others. It comes down to an attunement. We can all operate and work so much better with people who have a like mind rather than those who do not.

Q9   Do physical mediums suffer with their health?

A9   Yes. Most of the well-known physical mediums have suffered with their health. All of the ones that I have read about and been in contact with have diabetes, and some have heart and other problems.

Q10   I have heard that sitters can experience a 'pull' in the solar plexus when in a séance, but I experience pains in the chest and back, as do some others. Why is this?

A10   This is an energy pull from the chakras, but as bones, muscles and sinews, connect our body what happens in one part does sometimes have an action felt elsewhere. Most 'pulls' come from the solar plexus and the heart areas.

Q11   What is materialisation?

A11   Materialisation is where the form of a person in spirit is manifested so that it becomes tangible. It is made up from ectoplasm. Ectoplasm is made up from the mucus and moisture from our orifices. In the circle of which I was the leader, 70% came from the medium, 10% each from my wife and I, and the rest came from the sitters.

      It should be mentioned at this point that there is a very good reason to ensure that the room used for physical work is absolutely clean. When ectoplasm is used, at the completion of the session all of the ectoplasm returns from where it came. If a room is dirty, then all that dirt will also be returned to people's bodies, which can be harmful.

Q12   Does the quality of mediumship change depending on the weather and location?

A12   Yes. Where we are and what the weather is like will change our outlook and attitude, therefore it will make a difference to our abilities. From experience, pleasant surroundings and a warm climate definitely help spiritual contact.

Q13 Does one have to take a shower and change all their clothes before sitting in a circle?

A13 It is preferable in an ideal world to be completely clean when working with spirit, also, using the same clothes (provided that they have been washed each time). Obviously there are some who cannot be clean and non-fragrant, but the idea is to ensure that there are no extra smells that we could carry, as we cannot then be aware of smells given to us by spirit.

Q14 How can I get to know my guides better?

A14 In exactly the same way as you get to know your friends better—by interaction. The more contact the better chance there is to understand and appreciate that person, be it in this world or the spirit world.

Q15 What is psychometry?

A15 Psychometry is used to understand more about either the owner(s) or where the object is kept. Using our senses, it is possible to gain a lot of information, including what the person looks like, their characteristics and much more. The object is usually held in the hand, although some people seem to get a better result by putting the object to their third eye (centre of their brow).

Q16 What is inspiration?

A16 Inspiration is the result of not having logical thought. It is an idea that is not prompted by reason, but can be a random thought. It can also be a thought that has been prompted by spirit, usually for the betterment of humanity.

Q17 I am not very well educated, and I have heard that spirits are attracted 'like to like'. Does that mean that I won't do very well at mediumship?

A17 Not at all true. There have been many uneducated people who have been excellent mediums. Like-to-like is more about other qualities to do with characteristics and personalities. Within the parameters of trance, uneducated people can speak in different languages and have a wisdom given that is not inherent in them.

Q18 To contact spirit, I am told to concentrate and also relax. How can I do both?

A18 First of all relaxation should be achieved using pleasant music and a comfortable, but upright, chair. Having relaxed the body and mind, then the mind needs to be channelled (concentrated) towards working with spirit. This is a controlled action of being aware of whatever communication spirit may impart.

Q19 What senses are used in mediumship?

A19 Essentially the five main senses that we all have. Over the years, and by trying to help in teaching, I have now said that there are 12 senses when working with spirit. These cover the original five, but added to those are a thinking aspect. For instance: I can hear plus I think I can hear. This doubles the original five, making 10. We all have a 'sixth' sense, making 11 senses. Seeing has not just two, but three aspects. The three are: as we see each other, seeing clairvoyantly and seeing spirit solid. This makes a total of twelve senses.

With this many senses to use, it makes the choices a little easier. If we are trying to get a contact with spirit, it gives a larger range within which to work.

Q20 How can I 'blank' my mind?

A20   I do not know anyone who can. If we regard our thoughts as a carrier wave, then it needs to be in the background, and on that can be put any spirit thoughts. Thoughts need to be subdued, not eradicated.

Q21   Why must I not cross my arms and legs in circle?

A21   Generally it is assumed that we cover our working chakras when we either fold our arms or cross our legs. My viewpoint is that if we are giving a message to another person, I do not care whether they have their arms folded or not. The reason is that my communication is with spirit, which I do not obtain via another person's chakras. The only time that other people's chakras are used is when we are getting information from someone else's body for psychic work, not spiritual.

Q22   Why do some mediums get mixed up with whom the message is for?

A22   This is usually due to lack of discipline or inadequate training. A medium that is competent will not usually get anything mixed up. There are times when for whatever reason, energies are low, which sometimes can be attributed to the audience, and the evidence is not as sharp as it could be.

Q23   What colour light should be used for transfiguration?

A23   Normally red is used, but there have been times when I have used green and blue. There are many other factors that come into play, and it is worthwhile to experiment. Different people have different perceptions.

REINCARNATION

Q1   Do people reincarnate, and if so, how?

A1   Yes. A decision is taken while in the spirit world as to whether more can be learned if incarnation takes place. As there are more possibilities to change oneself spiritually in the earthly world, then this is the reason. We then choose to whom we will be born. There are not a specific number of incarnations to be achieved. It is different for all of us.

Q2   If we reincarnate, do we decide to come back to this earthly life, or is it decided for us?

A2   I think that we have a choice, maybe taking advice from someone who has a greater understanding, but I think that the choice is ours alone.

Q3   Who decides our parents?

A3   The decision is not made by whether the parents are 'nice' people, but by the need of the souls, both of the parents and the child. I would expect that we alone could not achieve that decision.

Q4   Do the same family group reincarnate together?

A4   I believe that they do. I cannot say with any certainty that I am right, but it would explain a lot.

GLOSSARY OF TERMS

Aura	*The vibrational field that surrounds each person and other living organisms. It can vary between a couple of centimetres and a whole room.*
Angel	A spirit that administers to us.
Apport	An object that has been dematerialised from one place and materialised somewhere else by spiritual intervention.
Astral travel	The out of body travel by our soul in the sleep state.
Automatic writing	The production of writing by a person who is in an altered state of consciousness, and controlled by spirit.
Circle	A group of people who are (normally) under training to become mediums, or a group of people who are trying to contact the spirit world for a specific reason. There are usually two types of circle for the training of mediums:

Open circle, where anyone can sit to sample aspects of mediumship.

Closed circle, where specifically invited people meet on a regular basis to learn about the development of spirit communication.

Clairaudience — (Clear hearing). The ability to hear spirit communication.

Clairvoyance — (Clear seeing). The ability to use the 'third eye' in order to see spirit and their communication.

Clairsentience — (Clear sensing). The ability to feel information provided by spirit.

Death — The time when our soul leaves our body and returns to the spirit world.

Direct voice — A voice box is formed external to the mediums own voice box, and through that the voice of a spirit can be heard. It is very similar to the actual voice of the person before they died.

Discarnate — Without a body. Describes those in the spirit world.

Divine service — The programme usually consists of prayers, hymns/songs, a reading, an inspired talk and a clairvoyant demonstration.

Entity — A person in the spirit world.

Eternal progress — The ability for people who live in the spirit world to progress to a level of greater perfection.

Etheric	A non-material spirit body.
Guide	A person in the spirit world who is working with a person on the earth, to aid their spiritual progress in this world.
God	The force that most people accept, although often the concept is different. The Great White Spirit, Jesus and Buddha are some variations.
Inspiration	Impressions given to us by the spirit world for speaking and writing things that we would not normally do.
Instrument	The medium.
Incarnate	Living in a physical body on the earth.
Kirlean photography	A type of photography that can show auras of living things.
Lyceum	An educational system for children (and some adults) who wish to learn about spirit.
Magnetic healing	First introduced by Mesmer.
Materialisation	The formation of a body (either wholly or in part) made up from ectoplasm as a replica of the spirit person.
Medium	The person who acts as a switchboard operator between spirit and another person on earth.
Meditation	Sitting quietly to obtain a different atmosphere conducive to working with spirit, or to achieve a certain goal when using the mind.

Mediumship	The act of being a medium. It can be through the mind (mental mediumship) or physical (manifestation of spirit).
Message	A communication from spirit.
Naming Ceremony	Similar to a christening, but where a name is given from spirit, then known as the spirit name. Usually conducted by a Spiritualist Minister.
Personal responsibility	The responsibility taken by us for our thoughts, words and deeds to achieve a higher standard.
Physical phenomena	The demonstration of forces from spirit such as materialisation, spirit voices, apports and other physical acts, not controlled by us.
Psychometry	The ability to ascertain information through the senses of something that is not normally apparent.
Recipient	The person who receives a message from the medium.
Rescue circle	A group of people who meet to assist spirit beings who are uncertain of their surroundings.
Séance	A circle that is more to do with physical manifestation than teaching.
Spirit	A person who has left this earthly life and is now in the spirit world. They have died.
Spirit communication	Information given by spirit to a medium or others, via a medium.

Trance	An altered state of being, usually when a person is influenced by someone from the spirit world.
Transfiguration	The formation over the medium's face of a replica of a person from the spirit world. There are two ways of this happening. A mask of ectoplasm can be superimposed over the face, or something like a hologram can be formed a small distance from the face.
Transition	Moving from life to death (the spirit world).
Zener cards	A set of cards to test telepathy.

ABOUT THE AUTHOR

The author with his wife Eve

GENERAL:

22 years in the Royal Air Force as an aircraft engineer (instrumentation and electrical). Volunteered for the RAF in 1947. Retired from the RAF in 1969.

30+ years as a Technical Author, writing in all engineering disciplines (mechanical, electrical, electronic, pneumatic, hydraulic, refrigeration, photographic and optical).

At some time a Fellow of the Institute of Scientific and Technical Communicators, the South East Region Pistol Coach, a watch repairer, taught ballroom dancing (twice), editor of 6 in-house magazines and first editor of *Spiritual Lifestyles* magazine.

LIFE:

Born in 1929 with an average Church of England upbringing. Started searching for a personal belief at 16 because of disenchantment with the C of E pathway. Visited most variations of religious churches in England, but at 25 attended a spiritualist church and found what he had been searching for. At age of 35, while still in the RAF, changed his religion to spiritualist.

He married his first wife, Joan, in 1952, and they had three children, Sharon, Cheryl and Glenn. Unfortunately she died in 1978 of pancreatic cancer, at the age of 47.

He met his current wife, Eve, in 1981, and married in 1984. They have lived in Taunton and Bridgwater, Somerset. From 1981 until 1989 they worked as mediums in Spiritualist churches and centres throughout the South of England from Newquay to Bristol, and Brighton to Milton Keynes, with many places between and further afield.

After moving to Spain in 1989 and then to the Netherlands the following year, they eventually returned to Sussex and settled in Crawley in 1993. They carried on their spiritual work, which included running the Sunshine (Spiritual) Centre in Crawley. Colin Fry has worked there.

Many mediums have also demonstrated in their home, including Tony Stockwell and other competent demonstrators.

Gordon is a certificated Healer, certificated Medium, certificated Counsellor and was Ordained as a Minister in 1998. He is also an officiant at funerals (both cremations and burials), naming ceremonies, wedding blessings and has carried out exorcisms. He has taught mediumship and healing in Holland, Germany and Denmark, and has also worked in Spain and America as a medium. He has run two-year courses on Healing in the UK and Denmark. He visited Denmark twice a year. In the capacity of an ordained minister he carried out the ordination of his best friend, Joern Tander. Both Gordon and his wife have run development circles since 1982, and additionally Gordon has been circle leader for David Thompson the physical medium.

Lightning Source UK Ltd.
Milton Keynes UK
UKOW032110101012

200388UK00001B/51/P